P9-DMF-241

THE SWAHILI

University of Pennsylvania Press

The Ethnohistory Series

A complete list of the books in this series
appears at the back of this volume.

THE SWAHILI

Reconstructing the History
and Language of an African Society,
800–1500

DEREK NURSE
and THOMAS SPEAR

University of Pennsylvania Press
Philadelphia

Designed by Carl Gross

Copyright © 1985 by the University of Pennsylvania Press
All rights reserved

Library of Congress Cataloging in Publication Data

Nurse, Derek.
   The Swahili: reconstructing the history and language
of an African society, 800–1500.

   Bibliography: p.
   Includes index.
   1. Swahili-speaking peoples—History. 2. Swahili
language—History. I. Spear, Thomas T. II. Title.
DT365.45.S93N87 1984   306'.089963   84-3659
ISBN 0-8122-7928-X
ISBN 0-8122-1207-X (pbk.)

Printed in the United States of America

Fourth paperback printing, 1995

CONTENTS

Maps

Figures

PREFACE

The history of the Swahili has long been tangled in the web of their own and other people's perceptions and misperceptions of them. At its most extreme, they have been seen as cultural aliens, Caucasian Arabs who brought civilization to a primitive continent. Just as state formation across the continent was seen as the product of Hamitic (Caucasian) invaders from the north, so the Muslim trading towns of the eastern coast were seen as cultural transplants from the Arabian peninsula. This view is not simply racist; it also implies an understanding of history that sees all cultural innovation in Africa as the result of diffusion of peoples and ideas from elsewhere, thus denying African historical actors roles in their own histories.

Our intention is to cut through this web by combining modern techniques of African historians with recent discoveries relating to the Swahili to portray their history. For all the interest in the Swahili language, few have attempted to reconstruct its historical development. Only recently have archaeologists turned their attention to the indigenous peoples of the coast and started to reconstruct the ways in which coastal towns and societies developed. Historians have tended to accept Swahili traditions pointing to Arabian origins at face value without seeking to discover what the traditions mean to the people who relate them. Finally, anthropologists have only recently started mapping the full dimensions of Swahili society and culture and the ways these relate to those of their neighbors.

This book has a message. We hope that it is argued convincingly and supported carefully, but lest it be misunderstood, let us briefly outline our argument here. Our basic point is that the Swahili are an African people, born of that continent and raised on it. This is not to say that they are the same as other African peoples, however, for in moving to the coast, participating in Indian Ocean trade, and living in towns their culture has developed historically in directions different from those of their immediate neighbors. It is also not to say that they have not borrowed freely from others. Arabs have been trading along the coast for a long time, and many have remained to settle and to become Swahili. They have influenced the development of coastal culture. But the influence has gone both ways, and the result has been a dynamic synthesis of African and Arabian ideas within an African historical and cultural context. The result has been neither African nor Arab but distinctly Swahili. It is this process we seek to trace.

The Swahili provide a laboratory unique in African history in the detail and the time depth over which we are able to use documentary, linguistic, archaeological, and traditional data, both to test the validity of each and to explore ways of combining them into a meaningful historical synthesis. We hope our attempt will be useful for other historians struggling with the implications of oral traditions, ethnographic data, or comparative linguistics in the more usual absence of supporting documentary or archaeological data and of absolute chronologies. Within the immense historical diversity and complexity of African societies, we all share the problems of method and of understanding.

ACKNOWLEDGMENTS

Our work has been made easier by and has benefited greatly from a number of recent and some not so recent studies that encourage one to view the history of the Swahili-speaking peoples in new ways. We trust our debt to them is made clear in the notes and bibliography. We would like to thank the following for facilitating our research, offering their ideas freely, and challenging ours: James de Vere Allen, Lee Cassanelli, Neville Chittick, Christopher Ehret, Mark Horton, Gillian Feeley-Harnik, Thomas Hinnebusch, Gerard Philippson, Randall Packard, Gill Shepherd, John Sutton, and Thomas Wilson. We would also like to thank the Institute of Swahili Research of the University of Dar es Salaam, the National Museums of Kenya, the British Institute in Eastern Africa, and the W. H. Whiteley Memorial Fund for supporting Nurse's research, and the National Endowment for the Humanities, the American Council of Learned Societies, and Williams College for grants supporting Spear's research and writing. Publication has been made possible by a generous grant from the President and Trustees of Williams College. The responsibility for what follows is, of course, ours.

DEREK NURSE
THOMAS SPEAR

I SWAHILI AND THEIR HISTORY

Dotted along the eastern coast of Africa from Somalia to Mozambique are a number of old Swahili towns (see map 1). Perched on the foreshore or on small offshore islands, their whitewashed houses of coral rag masonry crowd around a harbor where a few seagoing dhows are tied. Among the coral houses are a number of small mosques where men from the immediate neighborhood gather in their white gowns and small embroidered caps for prayers and outside of which they gather afterward to discuss town affairs in measured tones. Their wives and older daughters are not to be seen until evening, when, under cover of darkness and their loose, flowing black robes, they visit discreetly with their female relatives and friends.

The East African coast has long been involved in the wider world of Indian Ocean trade and culture. From early in the first millennium after Christ, dhows have sailed south from the Arabian peninsula and the Persian Gulf on the annual northeast monsoon to trade pottery, cloth, and iron tools for African slaves, ivory, gold, timber, shells, dyes, and perfumes, returning home after the monsoon winds shifted around to the southeast. Although African goods reached the Greco-Roman world before the third century and China by the seventh, trade during the first millennium was largely with Arab and Persian traders from Shirazi ports in the Persian Gulf. For much of the second millennium, however, East African trade passed to the Arabian peninsula. The first sign of the shift occurred in the ninth century with the rise of the First Imamate at Oman, but the focus of trade shifted permanently during the twelfth century to

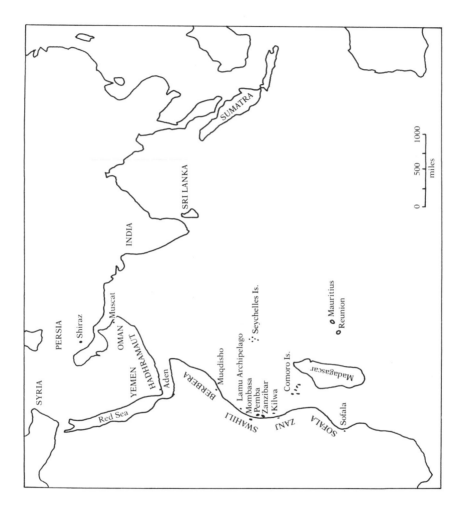

Map 1. Eastern Africa and the Indian Ocean

southwestern Arabia (Aden, Yemen, and the Hadhramaut) and, later, to Oman.

Most trade in East Africa itself during the first millennium was coasting trade, conducted on the beach between seafaring Arab merchants and African residents of the mainland. Only two market towns (Rhapta and Kanbalu) are known to have existed before 800, but we still do not know where they were located. The first permanent trading settlements that we can identify were established during the ninth century in the Lamu Archipelago (at Pate, Shanga, and Manda) and on the southern Tanzanian coast at Mafia and Kilwa. By the eleventh century, trade centered on Muqdisho in Somalia, where local dhows brought gold north from Mozambique and ivory, slaves, and other goods from elsewhere along the coast to trade with Arabs during the annual trading season. Muqdisho was noted in the thirteenth century for its wealth, size, and Muslim character, and Arabs had already begun to settle in the town. During the fourteenth century, however, Muqdisho lost its monopoly over the gold trade to Kilwa, located nearer to the gold fields at the southern limits of the monsoon trade. Kilwa continued to dominate coastal trade until conquered by the Portuguese in 1505, when the center of trade shifted north again to Mombasa in the fifteenth century and Pate-Lamu in the sixteenth. Trade and the coastal towns were badly disrupted during the sixteenth and seventeenth centuries by ongoing Portuguese raids and conquests until Oman defeated the Portuguese late in the seventeenth century, initiating two centuries of Omani Indian Ocean dominance, which culminated in the establishment of the Omani sultanate at Zanzibar and the extension of Omani power and cultural influence to towns all along the coast during the nineteenth century.

Though the Muslim maritime towns of the coast were not exceptional by themselves, they contrast with the rest of eastern and southern Africa. The Swahili language is spoken in towns scattered along two thousand kilometers of coastline, while their neighbors on the mainland speak dozens of different local languages. In the drier areas of Kenya and Somalia to the north, these neighbors are pastoralists, herding cattle, camels, sheep, and goats, whereas in the more fertile areas of southern Kenya, Tanzania, and Mozambique they raise maize, eleusine, millet, and sorghum together with various fruits and vegetables and small numbers of livestock. The peoples of the mainland rarely live in concentrated villages and never in coral houses, preferring to construct their thatched mud and wattle houses among the fields they farm or to erect simple temporary shelters as they migrate with their herds. And until recently very few were Muslim; most respected the spirits of their own particular lineage and clan ancestors.

Coastal Swahili-speakers have long stressed the differences between themselves and their neighbors, emphasizing their descent from immigrants from Shiraz in Persia and from Arabia who had come centuries earlier to the African coast to trade and who stayed to settle, build coral towns, live a sophisticated urban life, and rule. Later, when Omanis established themselves in Zanzibar and sought to impose their rule over the coast, Arabs exerted strong economic and cultural influences. Trade boomed, and during the prosperity that followed merchants from the Hadhramaut in southern Arabia became prominent community leaders, immigrant *sharifs* reformed and revitalized coastal Islam along contemporary Arabian lines, and people built elegant houses copying current Arabian and Indian features.

Thus, when Europeans visited the coast in the nineteenth century, Swahili towns appeared to be products of a Persian and Arabian diaspora that had spread around the Indian Ocean. The towns were not then very numerous or very large, numbering no more than a dozen containing a few thousand inhabitants each, but abundant evidence was found in ruins all along the coast of a vibrant period of Swahili civilization in the fourteenth and fifteenth centuries, marked by extensive and elaborate building and large-scale imports of Islamic and Chinese pottery, that lasted until the Portuguese destroyed a number of towns during the sixteenth century in their attempt to monopolize Indian Ocean trade. With the loss of trade, the coast went into decline until the eighteenth and nineteenth centuries when the Omanis initiated a new period of prosperity and of Arab influence.

The marked Arab appearance of the coastal towns, in contrast with the villages of neighboring Africans, and the claim to Arab and Persian origin made by the Swahili themselves have long led historians to portray coastal culture as an alien Muslim civilization divorced from the cultures of indigenous Africans, "strange foreign jewels on a mournful silent shore." Writing in the 1890s, Justus Strandes observed of Mombasa:

Shirazi Sheikhs are described as the earliest rulers, and according to the *History of Kilwa* found by the Portuguese, Muhammad the son of Ali bin Hasan, the founder of Kilwa, is considered to be the first of the line. These written accounts are confirmed by the verbal traditions of the native inhabi-

tants. Many buildings now lying in ruins are characteristic of Shirazi building. Even today the inhabitants of whole villages like to boast of Shirazi
descent. The fact that it is generally the chiefs, or the village notables, members of the ruling families of the past, who usually describe themselves as
being descendants of the old Persian emigrants, confirms the credibility of
the claim. As is natural, the centuries which have passed, and the continued
intermarriage with the native African have done much to efface the characteristics of the original stock. They are not, however, pure Bantu and it is
indeed remarkable how frequently the Aryan physiognomy and bearing dis-
tinguishes these people from the Africans amongst whom they live.[1]

Though archaeologists digging in the ruins of coastal towns
found little specific evidence of Persian influence, they continued to
emphasize the foreign nature of coastal civilization, attributing
basic architectural styles and subsequent innovations to Arab
inspiration.

The religion was Islam and the fundamental bases of the culture came from
abroad. In language and the materials of everyday life local African influence was stronger. The standing architecture however reflects little African
influence and its forms are entirely alien to those of the hinterland—its
origins were outside East Africa and it is present fully fledged in the earliest
known buildings. If anything, only a slow subsequent decline can be traced
in both design and technique. Nevertheless, the resulting style is individual
to the coast and homogeneous throughout its length. The culture was pro-
vincial—initiative was always from abroad.[2]

Similarly, linguists stressed the large number of Arabic words in
Swahili and the use of Arabic script in writing Swahili, while eth-
nographers wrote of the Muslim basis of Swahili society. The overall
message was consistent: "These cities of the coast look out over the
ocean; their society was primarily Islamic, and their way of life
mercantile. . . . We should picture this civilization as a remote out-
post of Islam, looking for its spiritual inspiration to the homeland of
its religion."[3]

Recently, a number of discoveries and revised perspectives have
begun to reveal the deep indigenous bases of Swahili culture and
history. Archaeologists have begun to analyze more closely the evidence for the early period of Swahili history between ca. 800
and ca. 1100 before they began trading extensively, building in coral
rag, and converting to Islam. Linguists have shown that Swahili is
clearly an African language, closely related to the Bantu languages
now spoken along the northern Kenya and Somali coast, and that it

has acquired much of its extensive Arabic vocabulary only in the last few centuries. Anthropologists have started to expand their studies from the cultures of the towns to those of Swahili fishing villages and mainland neighbors to uncover basic features of Swahili culture that reflect wider regional patterns. And historians are now reassessing documentary accounts and Swahili oral traditions in the light of these discoveries to reconstruct the local history of the Swahili that underlies the Arab veneer. These discoveries have fundamentally revised our view of Swahili history, so it is important to examine them and the implications they have for that history carefully.

The Swahili Language

Much of the traditional view of the origins and status of Swahili is captured by the following extract from a Nairobi newspaper:

History has it very clearly that Swahili is a combination of more languages than one, the major one being none other than Arabic. When the Arabs came to the East Coast of Africa before the exploitation era and consequently colonized it, they had no way of communicating with the indigenous people they met. Gradually and inevitably they tactically (and rightly so) combined what of their language they could with the languages that were being spoken there. There were many and still are—Giriama, Banjuni [sic], Digo, etc., not to mention those spoken further north and south of the East Coast of Africa. The result—Swahili. Some of the most prominent words in the language owe their origin to Arabic: salamu, salama, chai, lakin, etc.[4]

The first, and most obvious, fallacy here is that the most important feature of Swahili is its Arabic component. This feeling is widespread in both popular and academic writing and takes many forms. It is akin to saying that English, a Germanic language, is really a Romance language because of French influence during the centuries following the Norman invasion. This feeling is distorted because it fails to distinguish between what is inherited in a language and what is absorbed later. Swahili is clearly an African language in its basic sound system and grammar and is closely related to Bantu languages of Kenya, northeast Tanzania, and the Comoro Islands, with which it shared a common development long prior to the widespread adoption of Arabic vocabulary. Though some Arabic words were assimilated into Swahili before A.D. 1500, most are attributable to the post-Portuguese period. The Arabic material is a recent graft onto an old Bantu tree.

The second fallacy is that a single language arises in different places and, presumably, at different times: the Arabs "tactically . . . combined what of their language they could with the languages that were being spoken there." This view sees Arabic as a catalyst, which, on coming in contact with any available coastal language, ineluctably turned it into a form of Swahili. Another variant of this fallacy, while denying that Arabic was the catalyst, nevertheless sees Swahili as arising simultaneously at several different points along the coast. This polygenetic view of Swahili contradicts what we know from countless other languages in the world. A language arises in one place, over a period of time. Its speakers multiply, and the language starts to diversify internally. Its community splits up and some of its speakers move away, thus increasing the linguistic differentiation. It was during this stage in the history of Swahili that Arabic intervened. A language is created in a specific area and time, which is not to be confused with its subsequent development and differentiation.

The final objection to the view expressed in the quotation is the confusion of people and language. Most outsiders coming to the coast are usually struck by the images evoked in the opening paragraphs of this chapter, with their suggestion of foreign dress, religion, buildings, way of life, and even physical appearance of the people. From there it is an easy step to assume that the language of these people is also swamped with foreign elements. Though we do not deny that language and culture are intertwined or that foreign elements have been absorbed into the Swahili language, it behooves us to avoid any simplistic association of linguistic and nonlinguistic habits and to look more carefully at what in the language is Bantu and what is not, and how and when this non-Bantu element appeared.

Much of the distortion of the nature of Swahili is due to the lack of serious debate about the historical background of Swahili. Though there has always been considerable interest in the Swahili language, this largely concentrated on Swahili literature and, more recently, on the development of the language as a lingua franca for Tanzania and Kenya. Little interest was shown in its historical development, and that focused largely on the allegedly Swahili words quoted by early Arab travelers and on the language used in the earliest Swahili literature. But since the words cited by the Arabs are few in number, unreliable in form, and often present in neighboring languages, it is difficult to determine if most were in fact Swahili. Similarly, the evidence for the language of older Swahili literature is negligible.

Most Swahili manuscripts date from the last two centuries, a very few possibly from the seventeenth century. Swahili literature was essentially oral, and manuscripts were handed from scribe to scribe, each of whom felt justified in revising vocabulary, content, grammar, and dialect features in accord with current practice. Little was fixed. In addition, there arose a stylized convention for the language of verse, which in the last few centuries was based on the dialect of Lamu. The result is that very few manuscripts have reached us in a form of Swahili ascribable to a period earlier than the eighteenth, or, possibly, the seventeenth century. When we consider that the first signs of Swahili appeared in the ninth century, it is obvious that the language of the manuscripts has limited historical value.

Languages develop when people speaking a common language become separated from one another. In time the speech of each community changes, evolving into different dialects and eventually different languages. The problem linguists face in studying this development, however, is that they must start with languages currently being spoken and, by comparing these with one another, establish their relative commonality and reconstruct a probable pattern for their earlier development. The evidence for Swahili exists on several levels. On one, there are the different dialects of Swahili spoken along the coast, which can be compared to reconstruct the most recent periods of Swahili linguistic development. On a deeper level, Swahili as a whole can be compared with related Bantu languages to reconstruct the early development of the language itself. And, on a much deeper level, these Bantu languages can be compared with successively more distantly related Bantu languages spoken throughout sub-Saharan Africa to reconstruct the development of Bantu as a whole.

Historical linguistics is thus fundamentally different from history or archaeology. The historian or archaeologist usually deals directly with the evidence of the past in documents or material evidence that is contemporary with the period he or she is studying and hence is frozen in time, but languages are continually evolving. Since earlier forms of a language rarely exist except for written languages, linguists must start with present forms to draw hypotheses about their earlier stages and about the communities that spoke them. Historical and archaeological data are primary and direct, but linguistic data are secondary and derived from the historical languages we seek to study and hence are often felt to be an inferior source for history.

This underestimates the tools that a linguist can bring to bear on the data. As languages evolve, they not only absorb new material and develop new patterns, they also preserve inherited material in a solid base transmitted faithfully from generation to generation. The most obvious linguistic form is the word. When people encounter a language related to their own, what usually strikes them first is the similarity of many of the words and the difference of others. This is not an accident. Within any language community there is both a large common vocabulary and residual differences of vocabulary that result from such factors as age, sex, class, and occupation. When a language community splits up geographically, such differences increase. This happens when the split is total, such as when English-speakers migrated across the Atlantic, or gradual, as in the case of Gikuyu-speaking farmers in central Kenya who moved slowly over centuries farther and farther away from their original settlement area. It also occurs as some speakers come in contact with people speaking other languages and begin to use some of their words. Thus dialects develop by internal differentiation, by geographical distance, and through contact with other languages. Old words are replaced by new ones and drop out of use or take on restricted meanings. As the dialect communities resulting from the original split progress through time and expand in space, they change more and more, becoming less similar to each other, and at a certain point they become recognized as distinctive separate languages. Despite the lexical differences that develop, however, all the daughter languages retain some vocabulary that their speakers recognize as being similar, even though it may have changed in some ways.

Linguists have developed ways of quantifying these differences. If the vocabularies of two or more languages (D and E in fig. 1) are relatively similar, as measured by the percentage of common vocabulary they share, we assume this is because they have diverged only recently from a single parent community (B) and so have had little time to acquire new words. If we find another related language whose vocabulary is less similar (C), we assume that the split between B and C occurred farther back in time, thus allowing more differences to develop. D and E thus represent similar contemporary languages or dialects—two dialects of Swahili, for instance—whereas C is a less similar contemporary language. B represents an intermediate hypothetical language, or protolanguage, that we use to account for the similarity of D and E—proto-Swahili, for instance. A is the protolanguage that we use to account for the similarity of B, C, D, and E.

Some parts of vocabulary are more affected by changes than

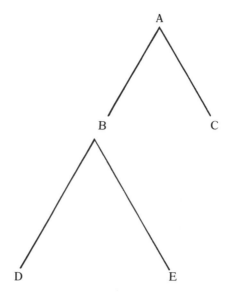

Fig. 1. Sample Language Tree

others. "Basic vocabulary," referring to familiar objects, natural phenomena, parts of the body, and common daily activities, is not very subject to change, whereas "cultural vocabulary," referring to specific cultural or technological items, tends to be replaced more quickly. Relative similarity in vocabulary between two or more related languages can be established by counting the number of common items in a standard list of basic vocabulary. The degree of similarity between related languages can then be expressed as a percentage and represented in a diagram such as figure 1, where the vocabularies of *D* and *E* were, for example, 80 percent similar, but those of *C* compared to *D* and *C* compared to *E* were only 60 percent similar.

Assessing the degree of lexical similarity between languages is not always a simple task, however; it depends on one's judgment of specific similarities between different sets of words. Compare the following sets of words from languages *D, E, C,* and *F:*

	D	*E*	*C*	*F*
"cold"	*bari̱di̱*	*baridi*	*baridi*	*baridi*
"vomit"	*-tapika*	*-tapika*	*-raβika*	*-chapika*

On the surface the words in the first line seem more similar than those in the second line, but the latter are in fact more significant. This is because the words in the first line are all recent borrowings from a single outside language whereas those in the second are all derived regularly from protolanguages *A* and *B* and are thus inherited items. And, since we wish to measure the degree to which related languages have diverged from a common root, it is the inherited items that are more important.

The claim that the similarities in the second line are more significant than those in the first is connected to the second tool that the linguist uses for measuring relatedness, that of sound changes. Sound changes are central to language change. Any sound in a given language may change, and when it does the change normally affects every occurrence of that sound in the language. Though the actual process of change is rarely observable, the results are clear when it has finished. The change of /t/ to /r/ to /ch/ in the second line takes place not just in this word but in hundreds of other words in these languages, as we can see:

	D	E	C	F
"bow"	*uta*	*uta*	*ura*	*ucha*
"tremble"	*-tetema*	*-tetema*	*-rerema*	*-chechema*
"tree"	*muti*	*mti*	*mri*	*nchi*
"fire"	*moto*	*moto*	*moro*	*mocho*
"three"	*-tatu*	*-tatu*	*-raru*	*-chachu*
"clasp"	*-fumbata*	*-fumbata*	*-fumbara*	*-fumbacha*

Since two of the four dialects have a /t/ sound, we can assume that protolanguages *A* and *B* also probably had a /t/ sound that changed to /r/ in *C* and /ch/ in *F*. If, on the other hand, we were to posit that the original sound was /r/ or /ch/, the sound would have had to change in all three of the other languages. Thus it is more economical to assume /t/ was the original sound, as exemplified in figures 2 and 3.

We can now refine our notion of similarity between words in related languages. If such words not only have the same or similar meanings but also show sound correspondences found widely throughout the languages in question, we say they are "cognate." Cognation gives us a more principled basis for determining the degree of relationship between vocabularies and languages than mere similarity and enables us to see how words derive from an original protolanguage. We can now say that *muti, mti, mri,* and *nchi* are cognate and derive from a reconstructed protoword **muti.*

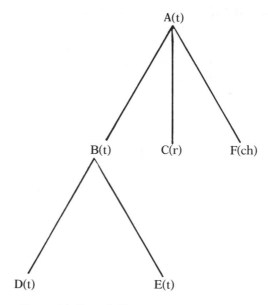

Fig. 2. Language Tree with Sound Changes

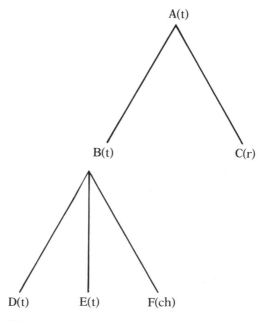

Fig. 3. Variant of Figure 2

We can also say that languages *D* and *E* are genetically related, that *D* and *E* derive from protolanguage *B*, and that *B* and *C* derive from protolanguage *A*, but we still cannot say whether *F* derives from *A* or *B* without further evidence.

Such sound changes and the regular correspondence of sounds between languages that result are important not merely in providing a basis for cognation but also as another classificatory device in their own right. Each set of regular sound correspondences between languages or dialects can be superimposed on one another to produce a general picture of similarity between the languages compared. The more similarities of either sound or vocabulary two languages or dialects share, the more likely they are to be closely related and to derive from the same protolanguage over a relatively short period of time.

Finally, linguists consider innovations in grammar significant for linking languages to each other and to a common ancestor, but the status of such innovations is often harder to determine. To take one example, we find that all Swahili dialects indicate the future tense by the infix -ta-, -ta-, or -cha- as follows:

Bajuni (N. Kenya): *chu-ta-kula,* "we will eat"
Stand. Swahili: *tu-ta-kula*
Vumba (N. Tanzania): *ru-cha-kŭlya*

Dialects of Comorian also indicate the future by a cognate form -tso-, as in *ri-tso-lima,* "we will cultivate." Although it would be possible to say that Swahili and Comorian developed these forms independently of one another, the simplest explanation is to say that at some point in their development they shared a common period of evolution during which this innovation took place.

We have been dealing so far with widespread similarities between languages that are the result of inheritance and divergence from a common protolanguage. But such similarities can also arise from convergence, or borrowing of words, sounds, or grammatical elements from one language by speakers of another, as in the case of *baridi,* "cold," above. Since borrowing usually happens when speakers of the two languages interact closely with one another and often involves distinctive clusters of related vocabulary, such as related words for ironworking or cattle keeping, we can deduce which language communities interacted in the past, how intensive that interaction was, and what sorts of practices were learned by one community from another from the evidence of convergence. Convergence may occur at different levels of language and may result from a variety of circumstances. One is the kind of influence that classical Latin and Greek exercise on the formation of modern scientific terminology or that English exercises on many languages today. Here there is little or no direct contact between the two language communities, but there is a degree of bilingualism on the part of at least some of the speakers of one of the languages. Another circumstance promoting convergence is regular contact between two adjacent language communities whereby trade, intermarriage, and bilingualism promote growing similarities between the two languages. A third circumstance is where one large or prestigious language community absorbs another but is itself changed in the process. The last two have always been common in East Africa.

The most obvious level at which borrowing takes place is that of vocabulary, or "loan words." Swahili today absorbs loan words from English and in turn exerts an enormous influence on the vocabularies of other languages in East Africa. But in the past Swahili borrowed widely from neighboring African languages as well as from Arabic, Persian, and various Indian languages. All Swahili dialects were greatly influenced by the assimilation of considerable numbers of speakers of other languages. As languages absorb large numbers of loan words, other levels can be affected as well. At first, for example, a language is likely to replace foreign sounds in loan words with its own more familiar sounds, but if borrowing continues on a large scale it is likely ultimately to adopt the foreign sounds as well. We can see this process in Swahili today. Whereas coastal communities long accustomed to the sounds of Arabic use /th/, /dh/, /gh/, and /kh/ regularly, other speakers to whom these sounds are alien replace them with /s/, /z/, /g/, and /h/. Even grammar may be influenced by outside pressure. In the past, Swahili poetic forms were heavily influenced by Arabic, and today Swahili syntax is being affected by English. At the same time, Swahili is spreading across East Africa, infiltrating other languages and actually threatening the existence of some of the smaller language communities. A few generations hence we will probably see a reduced number of languages in East Africa, but the casualties may well leave traces in regional forms of Swahili.

When loan words were accepted by a language can be determined by correlating them with sound changes. When a language absorbs loan words, they become eligible for any sound changes that occur after their absorption. Thus, if we can sequence the sound changes that have occurred, we can place loan words in that sequence by seeing what sound changes have and have not affected them. Let us take words of Arabic origin in Swahili, since they have given rise to such a variety of inaccurate and misleading claims. Arabic loans are clustered in various fields of cultural vocabulary relating to jurisprudence, trade, religion, nonindigenous flora, and maritime affairs. It is these specialized vocabularies that have led to statements that up to 50 percent of Swahili vocabulary is of Arabic origin. But the level of frequency of Arabic loans in basic vocabulary is very much lower. Some of the major sound changes that took place during the historical development of Swahili had already occurred by the beginning of the second millennium after Christ, and most were complete by A.D. 1500. Most vocabulary of Arabic origins has not been affected by these changes and thus is likely to have entered Swahili after 1500. The only sound change that affects Arabic loans to any extent is loss of the sound /l/. But loss of /l/ is very late in the sequence of Swahili sound changes and can actually be seen in progress in eighteenth- and nineteenth-century Swahili literature.

Additional evidence for the late adoption of Arabic loan words can be found by looking at the rural dialects of Swahili on Zanzibar and the mainland. These rural dialects still retain many pre-Arabic Bantu words, whereas if Arabic loans had been present for centuries they would have spread beyond the urban centers to replace these earlier forms. This is not to say that early Swahili did not borrow any vocabulary from Arabic. We know from early travelers' accounts that some words of Arabic origin were in use in Swahili by the twelfth century. But despite Arab presence on the coast since the first millennium, there has been remarkably little Arabic influence on Swahili vocabulary until relatively recently, suggesting that Arab influence was not very intense prior to the eighteenth century.

In summary, linguistics gives us a model for language development that can be related to other historical evidence. We can isolate groups of related languages and use them to posit the existence of earlier language communities that we can then relate to parallel lines of archaeological and historical data of historical peoples and cultures. We can reconstruct vocabulary for these protocommunities to identify features of their economy and general culture. And we can assess the nature of borrowing that has occurred between different language communities to determine patterns of interaction between different peoples in the past. In the case of Swahili we can identify its African roots and trace the general shape of its internal development from inherited material, and we can also identify African, Arab, and other influences on the language from loan words and other changes. Though historical linguistics can tell us that these events took place, it cannot tell us when or why they did so. For these we must seek additional information from other historical data.

Coral Rag Towns and Thatch Villages

Just as linguists once stressed the borrowed Arabic components of Swahili to the exclusion of the deeper genetic Bantu ones, archaeologists have tended to emphasize the alien Arab nature of Swahili material culture over its indigenous elements, as we have seen. Since no other people in the area built in coral and since the towns bore at least a superficial resemblance to Arabian towns, they reasoned, the art and architecture of the Swahili towns must have been an Arabian import. Similarly, the discovery of Islamic and Chinese pottery and of mosques in conjunction with early buildings led them to conclude that Arab traders and immigrants had been responsible for these new cultural developments. These conclusions were based on only part of the evidence, however. By placing such strong emphasis on the assumed discontinuous nature of the changes and on diffusion of ideas and people from Arabia as the causes of those changes, they neglected both the evidence for earlier periods of Swahili history prior to coral buildings and mosques and common patterns on different levels that reveal an evolutionary sequence of development.

Archaeologists are able to reconstruct past cultures on the basis of the material artifacts they leave behind and to distinguish between different historical periods in the different strata or layers as they dig down through the accumulated debris of the centuries. As one peels off the top layers or periods, one enters further and further into the past. Each layer of a site is part of a single period, and all the materials located in that layer relate to each other as part of a single cultural complex. If, for example, a layer contains local pottery, fish bones, sorghum pollen, postholes, and iron slag, we can deduce that it was a fishing and farming society whose members lived in mud and wattle houses and engaged in ironworking and pottery making. If imported pottery is also present, then trade probably took place. The materials from each layer can then be compared and sequenced with those from prior and succeeding layers to reconstruct a developmental sequence or relative chronology. Thus, if trade beads occur on one level and not on previous levels, we assume that trade, or at least a certain kind of trade, developed in that period. Finally, it is often possible to establish an absolute chronology through scientific dating of specimens taken from a level or through the knowledge that certain items found there were made in certain periods.

Pottery is the most easily identified and dated item found commonly in eastern Africa. Locally made pottery often shows distinctive shapes, techniques, and decorations in different places and at different times, thus allowing us to trace the spread of a particular style from one area to another or the development of a style through time. Imported pottery can easily be distinguished from local pottery because African pottery was made without a wheel and was always unglazed, suitable for cooking over an open fire, whereas imports were wheel-thrown and often glazed in particular glazes and designs known to have been made in certain places at certain times. Thus the presence of imports tells us not simply that trade took place, but also when and from where the items were imported, as shown below.[5]

Islamic		
Unglazed	9–12th c.	water jars, vases, ewers, jugs, and bowls
Sassanian-Islamic	9–10th c.	lead glaze in blue, green, brown, and yellow with symmetrical patterns
Tin-glazed	9–10th c.	white base with overglaze or painted decorations
Luster	9–14th c.	as above with second glazing; later types monochrome
Sgraffiato	10–13th c.	*simple:* scratched or incised design; *champlevé:* deeper carving in second slip
Chinese		
Celadon	13–16th c.	
Black-on-yellow, blue-on-white	14th c.	
Porcelain	14–17th c.	

The classic excavation of Neville Chittick at Kilwa provides a good example of the lessons we can learn from archaeology.[6] At the lowest levels Chittick found shells and fish bones, locally made unglazed pots, iron slag, grooved blocks used for manufacturing shell beads, together with great quantities of cowries and shell beads themselves, and a little imported Sassanian-Islamic and white tinglazed pottery. The earliest inhabitants, then, ate fish, worked iron, made pottery, and conducted some trade over the period ca. A.D. 800

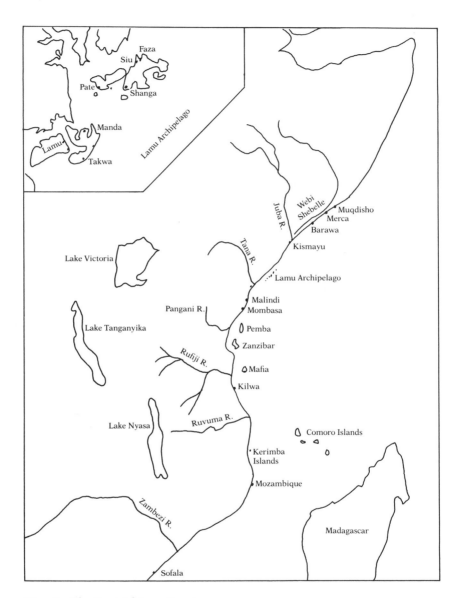

Map 2. The East African Coast

to ca. 1000. There is some increase in imports on the next level; now sgraffiato wares and steatite stone bowls from Madagascar dated ca. 1000 to ca. 1200 but, more importantly, postholes, red earth, and sorghum seeds provide evidence that people were living in rectangular mud and wattle houses on the site and farming. The first building in masonry was also undertaken at this time, using squared coral blocks set in mud mortar as foundations for mud and wattle houses. Between ca. 1200 and ca. 1300 dramatic changes occurred in Kilwa. Masonry houses and a mosque using coral blocks and lime mortar were built; imported glass beads largely replaced local shell ones; pottery making and ironworking continued while spindle whorls for spinning and copper coins were used; and imported pottery including Chinese porcelain was used in increasing quantities. Expansion of trade had led to considerable material development. From ca. 1300 to 1505, when the Portuguese sacked it, Kilwa enjoyed its greatest prosperity. Elaborate and extensive stone structures were built, including the domed extension to the mosque; Chinese porcelain became increasingly common, and local pottery underwent a marked change in style, while local spinning and ironwork appear to have ceased. Kilwa had thus developed over the centuries from a small local village to a great trading center, but the local element remained throughout. Local pottery continued to predominate, and mud and wattle building continued through all periods.

The significance of these finds is explored further in the recent excavations by Mark Horton at Shanga in the Lamu Archipelago.[7] Delineating twenty-one different phases, grouped into five periods, in the development of Shanga from ca. 850 to its abandonment ca. 1440, Horton shows in great detail the sequence of Shanga's historical development. The earliest levels, dated by the presence of Sassanian-Islamic, tin-glazed, and early sgraffiato pottery to ca. 850–ca. 920, contain evidence of ironworking, local pottery, agriculture, and some cattle herding but no clear indication of houses. These follow in Period II, ca. 920 to ca. 1020, with circular patterns of postholes overlaid by rectangular patterns, indicating that earlier round mud and wattle houses were later replaced by rectangular ones, while other activities continued and imported pottery remained rare.

A change in building styles occurred again in Period III, ca. 1020 to ca. 1250, with the use of squared porites coral blocks and mud mortar as foundations, into which poles were driven for wattle and daub walls, a technique that insured much greater permanence. Imported tin-glazed, Sassanian-Islamic, and early sgraffiato pottery are associated with the early layers here, porcelain and champlevé sgraffiato with the intermediate ones, and later sgraffiato, celadon, and black-on-yellow with the later ones. It is in this period that the first mosque was started, about 1120, using coral rag (rough-shaped blocks of coral readily available in the area) and mud mortar for walls in the initial construction. Later additions in Period IV (ca. 1250–ca. 1320) employed lime mortar and plaster to construct a more elaborate mosque with a vaulted timber roof, but dwellings in the same periods continued to be constructed of wattle and daub. Further additions to the mosque were made in the last period of Shanga's existence, ca. 1320–ca. 1440, with the replacement of the vaulted roof with a flat coral one supported on heavy cross timbers, but the most significant development in this period was the extensive use of coral rag and lime mortar in housing construction for the first time. One hundred and thirty-nine houses were built within the newly constructed town walls, and two mosques and a number of elaborate pillar tombs were also added. This was the peak of Shanga's prosperity, as also evidenced by the larger amount of imported pottery—celadons, porcelains, and Islamic monochromes—but the fall came quickly, and for no apparent reason Shanga was abandoned ca. 1440.

The lessons of Shanga, however, are more enduring. First, there was a clear continuity of development through all the periods as local pottery predominated and styles evolved organically. Building techniques slowly changed from mud and wattle to coral foundations, coral rag and mud mortar, and finally lime mortar and plaster. The town plan remained virtually unchanged, however, as later buildings were built on top of earlier ones. The sole exception was the mosque, where the pre-Muslim alignment of the building was altered slightly to face its *qibla* toward Mecca. These developments were largely independent of foreign influence. Though foreign trade, and presumably influence, existed from the beginning, the first uses of coral in building preceded the adoption of Islam, and subsequent developments were related more to local evolution with increasing prosperity than to the introduction of alien styles or technology. Lastly, and critically, the developments of Shanga can be related to those occurring elsewhere on the mainland and along the coast. The earliest-style local pottery at Shanga, and its association with ironworking, is directly mirrored some one hundred kilometers up the Tana River at Wenje, and the same style of pottery is found together with ironworking at the earliest levels of other coastal settlements at Kilwa, Manda, and the Comoros, linking Manda to a wider inland-coastal-island cultural complex.[8] The early Swahili were ironworkers who moved to the coast and began to trade their wares with foreign merchants. In the twelfth century it was noted that "iron is an article of trade and the source of their largest profits."[9] Shanga was thus an African town, first settled by local ironworkers, fishermen, and farmers whose increasing prosperity led to its slow transformation from a series of mud and wattle huts to a stone-built town over the course of six centuries.

When we compare sites like Kilwa and Shanga with others along the coast, a number of other lessons emerge.[10] First, those settlements that were later to develop into the largest and most prominent towns were all established at an early date, eight from the ninth to the eleventh centuries and another eight in the twelfth and thirteenth centuries. Though many more settlements were founded later, most of the later ones remained small or were short-lived. Second, while all were on the sea, the earliest were settled largely without regard to good harbors. Many were located on beaches or on creeks or islands with poor anchorages. They were thus primarily local settlements, and overseas trade was not a major consideration in their initial placement. Third, the earliest settlements grew up at both the northern and southern ends of the coast at approximately the same time, with Shanga and Manda in the Lamu Archipelago and Kilwa in the south all founded during the ninth century. Fourth, all developed at largely the same rate in conjunction with increases in trade, experiencing an initial period of expansion in the twelfth and thirteenth centuries followed by a burst of development in the fourteenth and fifteenth centuries. Finally, all of the settlements were fairly small by modern standards. The earliest settlements were mere villages; even at their peak in the fourteenth and fifteenth centuries, few were larger than forty acres and most were much smaller. Their populations must also have been small. Shanga had 139 masonry houses within fourteen acres; even allowing for a larger number of less permanent dwellings, the overall population could not have been more than a few thousand.

The main Swahili settlements were thus established initially as small, local farming and fishing villages developed at a number of different places along the coast. With the growth of overseas trade they underwent major expansion, culminating in the Muslim towns of the fourteenth and fifteenth centuries. The archaeological evidence thus provides us with a more detailed dated sequence of the early development of the Swahili-speaking peoples than the linguistic material, but it tells us little about the beliefs, social organization, politics, or ethnic origins of the people who actually lived in these villages or towns. For this we must turn to ethnographic descriptions of Swahili societies.

Swahili Society and Culture

Just as Swahili material culture has been seen as largely emanating from foreign sources, so other elements of Swahili culture and society have been viewed as predominantly the result of foreign influence. In the nineteenth century aristocratic families proudly bearing Arab *nisbas*, or family names, attributed their origins to prominent Arabian immigrants and ruled over the towns. *Sharifs*, tracing their descent from the prophet Muhammad, were prominent Muslim clergy, teachers, and lawyers. Literacy in Swahili using Arabic script and the ability to speak Swahili in a clever and sophisticated style and to compose poetry were highly valued. All these and more seemed to indicate cultured foreign origins in sharp contrast to the preliterate, small-scale, non-Muslim societies of mainland farmers and herders.

Ironically, however, there have been no detailed ethnographies of Swahili societies written until fairly recently to test these assertions. Recent ethnographies reveal a far more complex picture of indigenous development with reinterpretation and assimilation of foreign cultural features to fundamental Swahili ideas and values. Take the image of the Swahili town sketched in the opening of this chapter. What is omitted from this picture is the vastly larger number of mud and wattle houses surrounding the coral houses at the town center, and the farmers, fishermen, masons, carpenters, leatherworkers, and boatbuilders who live there. More importantly, it neglects to mention the dozens of small Swahili fishing and farming villages scattered the length of the coast, always greatly outnumbering the towns. In all of these life was more basic than the genteel Swahili life style would allow. Women could not afford to be secluded inside but had to work daily in the fields cultivating the crops and gathering firewood and water. Men had to rise at dawn to sail to the fishing grounds. Few were literate or claimed important *nisbas;* attendance at Quranic schools and prayers was low; beliefs in African spirits and witchcraft were common; and magic was practiced to protect crops and people—all in opposition to Muslim Swahili ideas while congruent with the values and ways of life of neighboring peoples. Thus, when we talk of Swahili culture we must bear in mind ranges of values and practices that varied according to wealth, status, and class.

At the core of every Swahili village and town were a number of named series of male and female descendants, matrilineages that passed from mother to daughter and patrilineages that passed from father to son.[11] Land was often held by corporate matrilineages of a mother and her daughters while political power, wealth, and status passed from fathers to sons. To prevent land, wealth, or status from becoming widely diffused, prominent families tended to intermarry, intertwining parallel matrilineages and patrilineages to keep land and power within a few interlocking families. Families and lineages came to be ranked hierarchically, maintained by the practices of preferential marriages and of restricting women from marrying down the hierarchy.

Villages and towns were divided geographically into wards. Since men tended to live with their wives' families upon marriage, each ward came to consist of one or more localized matrilineal groups of sisters and their interrelated husbands. Since families were ranked, so wards became ranked, primarily by wealth in land-holdings but also according to prestigious occupations and Muslim piety. Each ward was thus associated with certain families who were of similar status, worked together in common economic enterprises, worshiped at the same mosque, and interacted with one another on a daily basis. Each village or town was also divided into two sections, a northern half and a southern half, each including the wards and families within that half. One half was usually older and included the oldest and most prestigious families, the *waungwana*, who dominated political and religious leadership, while the other half included subsistence farmers and fishermen, Swahili from elsewhere, Arab traders, and neighboring peoples. Each individual was thus a member of a range of groups—lineage, ward, section, and town—that coexisted with others in states of complementary tension. An individual family or ward might dominate in political or religious leadership, in land ownership or production of certain crafts, or in trade, but each was linked to others in the interdependent context of the village or town economy, politics, and communal values and rituals as a whole.

The most important factor was land ownership and control over labor to work it, for these were fundamentally agricultural communities producing sorghum, millet, rice, coconuts, and various fruits and vegetables for consumption and trade. The most valuable land was usually the land around the village where valuable cash crops were grown. Village plots were frequently owned outright by *waungwana* families who produced perennial cash crops, settled people on the land to build up their own personal followings in village politics, arranged propitious marriages with other landowning families, and passed the land on to their sons. Land outside the village was controlled by matrilineal groups. Individuals who farmed it held use rights only and grew largely annual subsistence crops under shifting cultivation. Control over land thus lay at the roots of political power and status.

Less important both economically and politically was fishing. Though fish were an important part of the diet, no one could control their acquisition. Fishing thus tended to be the preserve of poorer people, who traded portions of their catch for other required commodities.

The third leg of the economy was trade, both internal and external. Local trade took place constantly among the farmers, fishermen, and craftsmen of the village and between village members and adjacent pastoralists, farmers, and hunters. Foreign trade was more limited and more concentrated, as merchants in the larger towns purchased stocks of ivory, sesame, ambergris, and mangrove poles from neighboring villages throughout the year in preparation for the brief annual trading season when the dhows arrived on the northeast monsoon from Arabia and the Gulf. As early as 1331, when Ibn Battuta visited the coast, such trade was often monopolized by a few wealthy merchants who took visiting traders into their homes and acted as their exclusive suppliers and agents. Wealth in the larger towns was thus controlled by large landowners and wealthy merchants, often the same people, who with their wealth were able to build extensive networks of followers in order to exercise political power.

Elders from the various families and wards sat on informal councils that the wealthier *waungwana* were able to dominate through their factions drawn from related wards, lineages, and families. In some cases such influence became translated into ongoing dominance by one or two families in monarchical fashion, but council representatives usually retained countervailing powers in responsibilities for ritual leadership and certain economic activities. Political power was thus centralized to varying degrees, from lineage and ward elders responsible for local affairs to representative councils and hereditary kings responsible for village or town affairs at large, and the greater the degree of concentration, the more elaborate the cultural and ideological supports for such social differentiation and stratification.

The most elaborate ideology was that of the *waungwana*, comprising the oldest and most respected families in the town. To be one of the *waungwana* one typically had to be a wealthy landowner, to trace one's descent from one of the earliest settlers in the oral traditions maintained for that purpose, and to live in a coral house in one of the more elegant wards. To have *uungwana* was to be "civilized" in the town mode: respected, credit worthy, dressed in the Swahili manner, and adept at Swahili verse. *Waungwana* jealously guarded their status through not allowing others to live in the central part of town or even to build in coral elsewhere, through maintaining long putative genealogies back to the original settlers, through restricted marriages with those of similar status, and through continual exercise of economic, political, and religious power over the town as a whole.

Islam also became an important component of this ideology. The wealthy endowed mosques and paid important clergy, secluded their women, sponsored elaborate *maulidi* celebrations to commemorate the birthday of the prophet, and built grandiose tombs to advertise their prominence; the poor attended the mosques of the wealthy, were less able to seclude their women, participated in *maulidis*, and continued to adhere to beliefs in the powers of ancestral spirits to insure the fertility of their land and their safety at sea. While distinctions in wealth were clear, those of belief were less so in practice. Subtle distinctions drawn between benevolent Muslim spirits associated with urban civilization (*jinn*) and malevolent spirits associated with the bush (*pepo*) were often ignored when disease or droughts struck, and both Muslims and traditional leaders practiced magic to overcome calamity. Similarly, the grandiose tombs of the *waungwana* not only attested to their greater religiosity but also advertised their power, wealth, permanence, and the prominence of their ancestors. Ancestor veneration through sacrifices and burning of incense was frequently carried out at the tombs for the well-being of the entire community.

What separated *waungwana* from other Swahili was not an absolute distinction but a gradient between two idealized cultural poles, the *uungwana* of the urban townsmen and the *ushenzi*, or "unculturedness," of the peoples of the hinterland, with most people occupying intermediary and often contradictory positions in the middle. Individual Swahili and Swahili societies were in a constant state of flux between the two, depending on their state of economic development. Never far removed from their rural roots in time or space, *waungwana* retained close links to them in their language, the importance of agriculture and fishing, and the religious syncretism that was coastal Islam. Villagers moved to towns and in times of increasing economic prosperity villages became towns, but when disaster struck townspeople returned to the countryside and towns reverted to being villages again.

Since Swahili societies were constantly changing, we cannot assume that the generalized model above, based on a number of different Swahili communities in the nineteenth and twentieth centuries, can be applied to any specific community in the twelfth, fifteenth, or even eighteenth century. Ideally, we could use documentary records of births, marriages, landholdings, and deaths to reconstruct earlier communities, but such records do not exist. What we must do, then, is to historicize the general model by seeking the antecedents of present practices and values in the linguistic, archaeological, and documentary data for earlier periods and for different towns. Reconstructed protovocabulary can indicate the relative antiquity of certain social and economic practices, such as farming and fishing techniques, specific rituals and beliefs, or common political procedures (see Appendix 7 for examples of proto-Swahili cultural vocabulary), and loan words can reveal the origin and timing of practices borrowed from others. Archaeological deposits also attest to earlier cultural patterns and reveal changes in them through residential patterns, tombs, ritual buildings and artifacts or through evidence of craft production and trade. And documentary accounts provide contemporary descriptions of earlier societies. By comparing such evidence for past practices with comprehensive descriptions of modern societies, it is often possible to reconstruct patterns of social and cultural development, identifying the changes and the continuities that are inherent in the historical development of societies and of cultures.

Cultural history is by nature a slow and evolving process of development as people face the problems of the present and future with the lessons and institutions of their past. Our aim is to build a dynamic model that combines what we know of specific institutions at particular places and times with known historical patterns in order to understand the main economic, social, political, and religious processes that made Swahili society what it was. We have seen, for example, that the expansion of certain towns, the development of social and political institutions, and the spread of Islam were all related to the growth of trade at different times and places along the coast. In the chapters that follow we will try to determine more precisely the processes of social and political development that underlay Swahili history.

Travelers to the Coast

Few historians have concerned themselves with tracing the roots of Swahili culture and the nature of its development. Most have been content to rely on early accounts of the coast by Arab geographers and travelers to trace the spread of an Arab diaspora on the assumption that Swahili culture and society were, in essence, Arab. That assumption is no longer valid in light of the linguistic, archaeological, and ethnographic evidence, and so the documents must be looked at anew in the light of the other evidence. Some historians have sought to synthesize the documentary and the archaeological evidence, and others have also used oral traditions, but none so far has brought all the evidence to bear on Swahili origins.

Although the documentary accounts relating to the coast from the second century appear to be the easiest evidence to use, they are difficult to interpret for a number of reasons.[12] All were by foreigners who collected their evidence at second hand or were in eastern Africa only briefly. The two earliest accounts, the *Periplus of the Erythraean Sea* (ca. A.D. 130–140) and Ptolemy's *Geography* (ca. A.D. 150), were both Greco-Roman collections gathered in Alexandria, and many of the rest were Arab compilations made in southern Arabia and the Persian Gulf. The notable exceptions were al-Masudi, who visited the coast ca. 915, Ibn Battuta, who stopped there in 1331, and a number of Portuguese accounts from the early sixteenth century. The rich detail of these accounts sets them off from the others and provides the majority of usable data. Those travelers who did visit the coast, however, were naturally attracted to the larger towns, and their contacts were limited to a few merchants or officials. The emphasis in the accounts is thus on politics, trade, and the foreign quarters where visitors stayed; rarely are we given detailed insights into wider Swahili society. Many of the references to places and peoples are also archaic and can no longer be identified. This is especially true of the earliest accounts; both the *Periplus* and Ptolemy place great emphasis on a town named Rhapta somewhere on the southern coast, and Masudi stresses Kanbalu, also in the south, neither of which has been located. Not until the Portuguese accounts of the sixteenth and seventeenth centuries is it possible to identify local ethnic groups, and even general discussions of local populations are often ambiguous.

Given these difficulties, then, what can we learn from these accounts? First, we learn something of the historical geography of the coast. The early concentration on Rhapta and Kanbalu indicates that trade was concentrated in the south throughout the first millennium. From the tenth century a more detailed knowledge of the coast slowly emerged, first of three main sections—Berbera (the Horn), Zanj (Muqdisho to southern Tanzania), and Sofala (Mozambique)—and then of particular towns and regions: Muqdisho, Barawa, Shungwaya, Swahilini (the Lamu Archipelago), Malindi, Mombasa, Zanzibar, Pemba, Kilwa, and the Comoro Islands. But this view was certainly not comprehensive. None of the towns of the Lamu Archipelago was specifically mentioned, for example, though Manda, Shanga, and Pate were certainly growing in prominence from the ninth or tenth century. The view was strongly biased in favor of major entrepôts of Indian Ocean trade to the exclusion of countless other towns and villages that dotted the coast.

The bias toward trade is clearly seen in the detail with which trade goods were reported. The basic exports of ivory, tortoise shell, and rhinoceros horn were first mentioned in the *Periplus;* later accounts added ambergris (ninth century); slaves, leopard skins, and gold (tenth century); iron (twelfth century); gum and myrrh (thirteenth century); and cotton cloth and grain (fourteenth century). Imports included lances, hatchets, swords, awls, glass vessels, wine, and wheat (second century); food and clothing (tenth century); and white cotton cloth, porcelain, copper, and red cotton (thirteenth century). Yet, strangely, no mention was made of Islamic pottery, which was one of the main imports. Trading practices were also carefully detailed. The *Periplus* first mentioned that traders gave gifts to establish goodwill prior to trading and that they frequently intermarried with the local people and spoke their language. In the ninth century, strips of cloth were given, and traders swore oaths of blood brotherhood. By the fourteenth century, an elaborate etiquette had developed whereby local traders met visiting merchants on their ships, offered them food, and then invited them into their own homes to conduct their business.

Compared to trade, we learn much less about the peoples and cultures of the coast. Peoples along the southern coast fished, using sewn boats and dugouts in the second century; those from Zanj had oxen, hunted and fished, raised bananas, millet, and root crops, collected honey, engaged in ironwork, and grew coconuts (ninth century). Politically, the *Periplus* noted that each settlement was autonomous, ruled by its own chief, and later accounts refer to kings and to Zanj capitals and kingdoms. Other evidence indicates that individual towns and villages remained largely independent of one another, however, providing an ambiguous picture of coastal politics.

Our knowledge of the coast is further confused by the question of the racial, ethnic, or religious identity of the coastal peoples. Rulers were frequently identified as Muslims or "Moors" and the local inhabitants were black, but the dichotomy was not that simple. First noted as black in the tenth century, frequent references to the Zanj (blacks) later confirm that the Zanj coast, at least, was largely populated by Africans. Subsequent references to Muslims, however, often confused race and culture. Masudi noted that Kanbalu had "a mixed population of Muslims and Zanj idolators" and went on to describe Zanj in terms that were clearly not Muslim. Islam was not mentioned in detail again until Battuta, a Muslim *qadi* himself, wrote extensively on coastal Islam in the fourteenth century. In Zeila, he noted that "the inhabitants are black, and follow the Shafi'i rite," but later he writes that "the people are dark-skinned and very many of them are heretics." In Muqdisho he stayed with the local *qadi*, attended the Friday mosque, noted the existence of large tombs, and remarked on the prominence of *sharifs* and those who made the pilgrimage to Mecca in the royal court. Masudi also made brief mention of mosques and Muslim piety in Mombasa and in Kilwa, "the greater part of whose inhabitants are Zanj of very black complexion."[13] It would appear, then, that there was not a sharp dichotomy between foreign Muslims and local Africans; the population was largely black, including many who had become Muslim by the fourteenth century.

A final lesson that we can learn from the documents is, perhaps, the most obvious. They provide us with a clear set of dates to establish an absolute chronology for developments along the coast, something only archaeology can also provide, though in a more generalized fashion. Archaeological dating refers to distinct periods of historical development; however, the dates of the documents are arbitrary, relating not to major historical events but simply to the time the documents happened to be written. Thus the documents give us some indication of the depth of coastal history and of the coast's long participation in the wider world of Indian Ocean trade but provide few benchmarks for the development of specific peoples, cultures, or towns of the coast. For these we must turn to the traditions of the peoples themselves.

Oral Traditions

The final sources for the early history of the Swahili are the oral traditions related by them about their own past. These traditions are of two main types. The first are family traditions, usually genealogies tracing descent from early settlers, often Arabs or Persians. The others are town traditions, tracing the history of the origin of a town, often in terms of successive waves of immigrants. Both lend themselves easily to an interpretation of foreign origins.

This interpretation is wrong for two reasons. The first is the changes in the traditions caused by the dramatic increase in Arab influence during the nineteenth century with the establishment of Omani rule in Zanzibar, causing a profound Arabization of local building styles, Islam, politics, and language, which was quickly reflected in increasing emphasis on putative Middle Eastern genealogical links in family and town traditions. The other is the failure by historians to take account of the dynamics of traditional thought. Taking traditions literally has been a common fallacy among historians, who fail to see that traditions both relate history and are history. In providing explanations and meaning to the people who relate them for their own cultural values and social institutions, they are an integral part of the history they convey. Traditions operate on two levels. On one they are models of society that convey abstract principles in concrete terms. Genealogies are not simply literal lists of ancestors, for example, but historical models that state and explain the development of social relations between people and through time in terms of a simple reproductive model. On another level, traditions are themselves part of history, providing models for social action, and as part of the action they become transformed by it. As social relations change, genealogies are manipulated to reflect the actual situation, thus explaining the widespread transformation of Swahili family names into Arab ones during the nineteenth century.[14]

Fortunately, however, these transformations did not completely erase the earlier traditions; often they were appended to them, so that we can dig through the accumulated layers of the traditions to discern several historical periods in the development of Swahili society. The first is often stated in terms of hunters who first inhabited the land, and the second by immigrants, the Shirazi, who gave the hunters cloth, married their daughters, and settled to become prominent Swahili families. These compose the essential *waungwana* myth and are fundamental to understanding the early development of Swahili society as something distinct from the societies of their neighbors. Successive periods recount further groups of immigrants, long lists of rulers, and ultimately the arrival of the Omani, and it was during this time that the particular Muslim and Arab bases of nineteenth-century society were established.

In highlighting the main periods and themes of Swahili history, the traditions accurately portray the historical development of Swahili society. Starting with the earliest inhabitants of the coast, they relate the growth of trade and subsequent development of economically differentiated and socially stratified societies whose cultural lexicon included some items that were foreign but whose cultural grammar was clearly African. In the final period, the foreign components of the cultural lexicon grew dramatically, providing the illusion of alienness, but our aim here is to look behind that illusion to the grammatical evidence that still exists for the African roots of the Swahili.

The linguistic metaphor is apt, for we shall start our inquiry with the origins of the Swahili language in the Bantu languages of equatorial and southern Africa. This is the protohistory of the Swahili, for people speaking the Swahili language emerged only at the end of the period. The earliest period of Swahili history, properly speaking, lasted from the ninth to the twelfth centuries, when people speaking the Swahili language spread down the coast of eastern and southern Africa to found numbers of small fishing, farming, and ironworking villages and to establish the basic foundations of Swahili society and culture. The second period includes the profound changes that took place in Swahili society and culture with the expansion of trade from the twelfth century until the effective destruction of coastal commerce by the Portuguese early in the sixteenth century, by which time the primary structures of Swahili society had become well established.

2 THE AFRICAN BACKGROUND OF SWAHILI

The Swahili language has undergone spectacular growth during the last century as a result of the language policies of colonial and independent governments, and today it is spoken by more than thirty million people throughout eastern Africa. Most of them now are second language speakers, but up to the nineteenth century Swahili was strictly a coastal phenomenon, spoken as a first language by people along the east coast of Africa from Somalia to Mozambique and the northern coast of Madagascar. The descendants of these people still speak Swahili today as their only language, and it is with these historical Swahili-speakers that we are concerned in this book.[1] But Swahili is only one of a large number of languages spoken in eastern Africa today, and its development is part of a large and complex linguistic history.

As long as twenty thousand years ago, perhaps earlier, eastern and southern Africa was widely occupied by peoples who lived by gathering and hunting and spoke languages known as Khoisan. Their presence was largely uninterrupted until just over three thousand years ago when new peoples came south from southern Ethiopia and spread over much of eastern Africa. These people, referred to as Southern Cushites, were farmers, herders, and hunters, and they interacted in various ways with the earlier Khoisan-speakers. In areas suitable for farming and herding, Southern Cushites assimilated the Khoisan communities or drove them out. In less suitable environments, the latter were largely left to their own devices.

A few centuries later, starting some twenty-five hundred years ago, increasing numbers of peoples speaking Bantu languages moved into East Africa from the west and southwest. As they were or became economically similar to the Southern Cushites who preceded them, they tended to occupy the same ecological niches. Thus, as they continued to move slowly east, they absorbed much from the Southern Cushites, both linguistically and economically, but over time Bantu-speakers overwhelmed the Southern Cushites and absorbed them. The linguistic diversity among the various Bantu-speaking groups was much less than now. But as linguistic, economic, and cultural differentiation became greater by early in the first millennium, we see the emergence of the ancestors of many of today's Bantu-speaking peoples. By about A.D. 500, the forebears of the historical Swahili, still essentially undistinguished from other very closely related peoples, had moved across East Africa to a position in the far northeast of the Bantu-speaking area, near the coast north and south of today's border between Somalia and Kenya. As small, incipient Swahili communities emerged in the middle and latter part of the first millennium along this northern coast, they had to contend with, and absorb, considerable numbers of people who were neither Bantu-speaking nor farmers, including earlier Southern Cushites, ancestors of the modern Dahalo; the Eastern Cushitic ancestors of the modern Aweera, who first arrived at the coast at much the same time as the early Swahili; and Arabic-speaking sailors trading along the coast.

The Non-Bantu Languages of Eastern Africa

The earliest identifiable language group in eastern Africa was Khoisan, whose best-known feature is the presence of click sounds. Khoisan languages are still spoken by small numbers of hunters and gatherers in southern Africa today, but their numbers there have been greatly reduced over the past millennium as Bantu- and Afrikaans-speaking farmers and herders expanded and pushed the hunters into ecologically marginal areas. A similar process must have occurred earlier in eastern Africa where Khoisan languages were once widely spoken as well. The evidence for this is twofold: the presence in many of today's Bantu languages of words taken from Khoisan languages, which points to historical contact between Khoisan- and Bantu-speaking communities, and the continued existence of isolated Khoisan languages in East Africa. The only language identified clearly as Khoisan is Sandawe, spoken in northern

Tanzania; but languages such as Hadza, also spoken in northern Tanzania, and Dahalo, spoken near the mouth of the Tana River in northeastern Kenya, show unmistakable signs that they had been in close contact with Khoisan-speaking communities or that Hadza- and Dahalo-speakers once spoke a Khoisan language themselves. Both Hadza- and Dahalo-speakers lived by hunting and gathering until the last decade, both have clicks in their language, and both are threatened with absorption into neighboring communities, following a general pattern that has doubtless been repeated over the past two millennia and that accounts both for the paucity of Khoisan communities today and for the widespread traces of their earlier presence in contemporary languages. It is impossible to date the first appearance of Khoisan peoples, but we assume that many of the Stone Age cultures that preceded the advent of the Iron Age late in the last millennium B.C. were Khoisan-speaking. They would therefore have been scattered throughout eastern Africa for more than fifteen thousand years prior to the arrival of farmers and pastoralists from the north speaking Southern Cushitic languages.

Starting in the third millennium B.C., growing population resulted in migrations into East Africa by Southern Cushitic–speaking peoples from Ethiopia (see fig. 4). During the second millennium B.C. Southern Cushites spread slowly down the Rift valley into the central Kenya highlands, where they arrived some three thousand years ago. In the course of the next millennium, this original group dispersed into many parts of Kenya and Tanzania, including Lake Victoria, large areas of western and central Tanzania, the Luguru Mountains, the Pare Mountains, the Taita Hills, Kilimanjaro, and down the Tana River to the Indian Ocean (see map 3). During this

Fig. 4 Southern Cushitic Languages

Family	Group	Subgroup	Languages
Cushitic: Southern	Mbuguan		Ma'a, Mbughu
	Dahaloan		Dahalo
	Rift	East Rift	Qwadza, Asa
		West Rift	Iraqw, Goroa, Alagwa, Burunge
	extinct	South Nyanza Taita Cushitic	

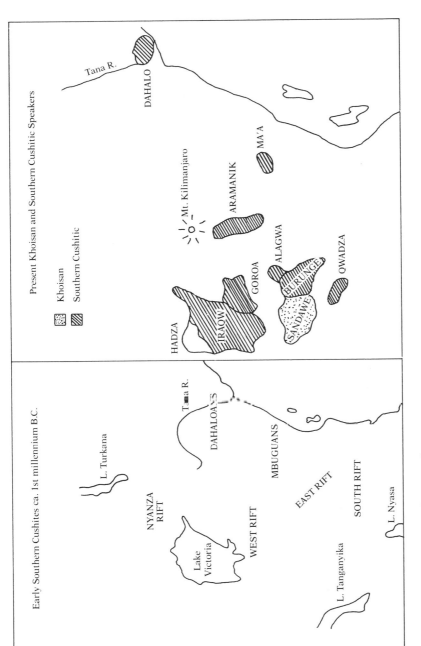

Map 3. Khoisan and Southern Cushitic

expansion they assimilated groups of Khoisan hunter-gatherers. The only Southern Cushitic–speaking group left on the coast, the Dahalo, is the result of such assimilation as their language retains a characteristically Khoisan click. Southern Cushites had become a major presence in eastern Africa by the first millennium after Christ, and they had a considerable impact on the economic activities of subsequent immigrants. Examination of archaeological sites, Southern Cushitic vocabulary, and modern Southern Cushitic communities in western Tanzania indicates that the early Southern Cushites were stone-tool-using herders and farmers, keeping cattle, sheep, goats, donkeys, and domestic fowl. They raised various types of grain, such as eleusine and sorghum, and probably ensete. It was likely that there was no clear distinction between food producing, food gathering, and hunting, for their vocabulary also reveals a knowledge of hunting with spear and bow and arrow.

Though at least three small Southern Cushitic groups have survived into this century by hunting in marginal lands, Southern Cushitic farmers and herders began to be displaced and absorbed by incoming Bantu-speakers over two thousand years ago. All have subsequently disappeared as distinct peoples, but they have left traces of their former existence in the large number of loan words absorbed into the Bantu languages during the period of interaction and assimilation in which Bantu-speakers came to predominate throughout eastern and southern Africa, a phenomenon we shall explore in detail shortly.[2]

Following the Bantu, cattle and camel herders speaking Eastern Cushitic languages related to Southern Cushitic began to infiltrate eastern Africa from the north (see fig. 5). The split between Eastern and Southern Cushitic occurred at least four thousand years ago, and their subsequent histories were quite separate. Some two thousand years ago there was a major Eastern Cushitic concentration around Lake Turkana in northern Kenya. By A.D. 500 the Eastern Cushitic ancestors of the Aweera had probably reached the coast of Somalia and later gave up herding for hunting and gathering, probably under the influence of the Dahalo. By the beginning of the present millennium, Eastern Cushitic Somali had also started to filter south into southern Somalia where, as we shall see, they interacted with northern Swahili communities in the first half of the present millennium. The final Eastern Cushitic group to impinge on the Swahili and related peoples were the Orma (Oromo), who pushed south out of Somalia into northeastern Kenya in the sixteenth century, disrupting coastal patterns established for over five hundred years.

Fig. 5. Eastern Cushitic Languages

Family	Group	Subgroup	Languages
Cushitic: Eastern	Lowland	Oromo (Galla)	Orma, Waata (Langulo, Sanye), Boran
	Omo-Tana		Somali, Aweera (Boni, Sanye), etc.

The language history of East Africa was thus a very busy one, with small groups of immigrants infiltrating the area, interacting with peoples already there, and frequently absorbing considerable numbers of speakers of other languages together with features of their speech. Khoisan-speaking hunter-gatherers were slowly absorbed by Southern Cushitic–speaking farmers and herders, but not before contributing to Southern Cushitic sounds and vocabulary in the process. Southern Cushitic–speakers were challenged in turn by Bantu-speaking farmers and herders moving from the west over a long period of time, while subsequent migrations of Eastern Cushitic–speakers from the north completed the modern language map of the area.[3] But it was the Bantu-speakers who were to emerge as the dominant group.

Bantu

Over four hundred Bantu languages are spoken by 130 million people today over the entire southern third of the African continent, and all are so closely related to one another that they must have spread rapidly throughout the area from the proto-Bantu homeland in Cameroon and eastern Nigeria over the past two or three thousand years.[4] The split between proto-Bantu and related languages of eastern Nigeria probably took place during the second millennium B.C. as proto-Bantu-speakers moved south and east into the equatorial forest, from which they subsequently emerged onto the southern and eastern savannas during the last millennium B.C.

The transition from the forest to the savanna was an important one for the Bantu because it forced them to change from a predominantly fishing and root crop economy to one focused on grain cultivation and stock herding. Cognate words widely distributed in

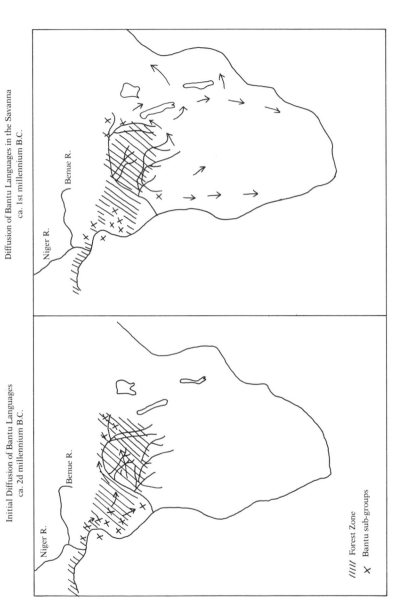

Initial Diffusion of Bantu Languages
ca. 2d millennium B.C.

Diffusion of Bantu Languages in the Savanna
ca. 1st millennium B.C.

Niger R.

Benue R.

Niger R.

Benue R.

///// Forest Zone

✗ Bantu sub-groups

Map 4. Bantu Expansion

Bantu languages today, words that must therefore derive from proto-Bantu vocabulary, indicate proto-Bantu-speakers hunted with bow and arrow and traps; collected honey and wax; fished with hook and line, nets, and baskets; paddled canoes; kept goats; molded pottery, water and storage pots; cultivated various root crops and palms; and ground or pounded their food—activities that were all closely associated with the forest environment in which they lived.

The Bantu languages of eastern and southern Africa today also have extensive vocabularies for grain cultivation, ironworking, and keeping stock that are absent from proto-Bantu, indicating that proto-eastern Bantu-speakers developed these activities after their arrival in eastern Africa but prior to their subsequent dispersion throughout eastern and southern Africa. In the case of grains it is clear that the change in environment mandated a change from forest root crops to savanna cereals. When Bantu-speakers first entered eastern Africa, Southern Cushites had already been there for nearly a thousand years, and they grew eleusine, sorghum, and probably ensete, which Bantu-speakers adopted as they moved into the area, taking the appropriate Southern Cushitic words into their vocabulary as well. They also adopted new livestock, including sheep, donkeys, chickens, and cattle, the words for all of which derive either from Cushitic or later Nilotic-speaking peoples.[5]

The data for ironworking are less easy to interpret. The proto-Bantu in their homeland were probably still in the Stone Age since the only two iron-related terms that are proto-Bantu are "to forge" and "hammer," and these could easily be the result of modifications of meaning from pre–Iron Age culture (e.g., "to forge" derives from "to pound"). Most other technical vocabulary has a regional rather than a universal distribution. Surprisingly, little of it is borrowed from non-Bantu sources. The variety of locally derived terminology indicates that they adopted ironworking after they had left their homeland and had started to filter through the forest and after proto-Bantu had already splintered into different offspring. We are not sure exactly how or when this diffusion took place; the earliest dates for ironworking are at Nok in Nigeria and Meroë in the Sudan, outside the Bantu area. Knowledge of ironworking thus probably diffused among the expanding Bantu so that by the time they were expanding in East Africa they had this newly acquired skill with them. The non-Bantu peoples present in East Africa before the Bantu migrations were not familiar with ironworking and seem to have acquired it at much the same time.

This interpretation differs from ideas current ten or twenty years ago when it was thought that Bantu-speakers had brought a wide acquaintance of ironworking and food producing with them from their homeland and that it was this knowledge, together with food plants such as banana and coconut that had infused from southeast Asia via the east coast, that enabled them to expand rapidly through eastern and southern Africa. Although Bantu-speakers did push rapidly south and east, we now see that they acquired major elements of their economy after the initial dispersal from their homeland. Crossing the equatorial forest they were hunters and fishermen, with limited knowledge of stock and food raising. By the time they reached the Great Lakes they were learning to smelt and forge iron, and soon after their arrival in East Africa they learned mixed farming as well.[6]

The Eastern Bantu

There is a problem reconciling the archaeological and linguistic evidence for the precise timing and movements of Bantu-speakers into eastern Africa. The earliest ironworking centers are found west of Lake Victoria, where there is evidence of iron smelting and an associated pottery type, Urewe ware, attributable to Bantu-speakers from the closing centuries B.C. A second series of sites, associated with a different type of pottery known as Kwale ware found in northeastern Tanzania and southeastern Kenya, dates from around the second century after Christ, indicating a diffusion of ironworking east from Lake Victoria to the Kenya coast early in the first or second century. Linguistic evidence, however, indicates that Bantu languages spread from south of Lake Tanganyika northeasterly toward the Kenya coast since the languages spoken at the northeastern extremities of Bantu expansion are more closely related to the languages of southwestern Tanzania and northern Zambia than they are to the languages spoken around Lake Victoria.[7] It may have been that, while one or more groups of Bantu speakers slowly infiltrated eastern Africa from south of Lake Tanganyika, others entered north of the lake. In this case, it was the later groups who possessed knowledge of ironworking, which then diffused separately to eastern Kenya.

However the conflicting archaeological and linguistic evidence is resolved, four major Bantu groups developed subsequently in the northeastern area: Rufiji-Ruvuma, Chaga-Taita, Thagicu, and Northeast Coast (see fig. 6). Rufiji-Ruvuma is spoken by peoples

Fig. 6. Northeastern Bantu Languages

Family	Group	Subgroup	Languages
Bantu: Eastern	Rufiji-Ruvuma	Rufiji	Rufiji, Ndengereko, Matumbi, Ngindo, Matengo, Mpoto, Manda, Ngoni
		Ruvuma	Yao, Mwera, Makonde, Maviha
	Chaga-Taita	Saghala	
		Dawida	
		Chaga-Gweno	West Kilimanjaro, Central Kilimanjaro, Rombo, Gweno
	Thagicu		Sonjo, Gikuyu, Meru, Kamba, Daisu
	Northeast Coast	Pare	North Pare, South Pare, Taveta
		Sabaki	Elwana, Swahili, Pokomo, Mijikenda, Comorian
		Seuta	Shambaa, Bondei, Zigula, Ngulu
		Ruvu	Gogo, Sagara, Vidunda, Kaguru, Luguru, Kutu, Kami, Zaramo, Kwere, Doe

today living in southern Tanzania and northern Mozambique in the lowlands between the Rufiji and Ruvuma rivers. The fact that these peoples have largely retained a proto-Bantu economy, with only the addition of grains and ironworking; that they were scarcely concerned with cattle; and that they acquired few loan words from Cushitic or Nilotic languages indicates that these peoples largely avoided the fusion of Bantu and non-Bantu elements that occurred to the north. The lack of homogeneity in Rufiji-Ruvuma vocabulary and the general shape of the geographical area they now cover make it likely that they started to move toward the Indian Ocean early in the first millennium after Christ, though the details of this spread are not clear.

The dialects of Chaga on Kilimanjaro, Gweno in North Pare,

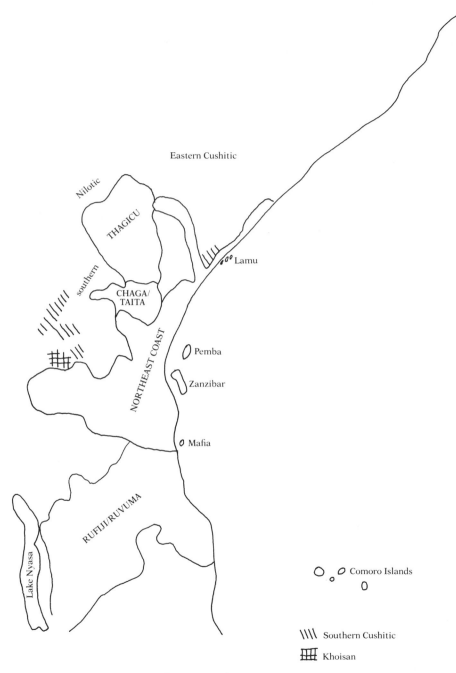

Map 5. Bantu Languages of Eastern Africa

and the Taita languages compose Chaga-Taita, spoken exclusively today in the mountains along the Kenya-Tanzania border. The degree of differences between these languages and the presence of early archaeological sites in the mountains indicate a proto-Chaga-Taita community early in the first millennium after Christ, perhaps in North Pare, whence they migrated to the Taita Hills and Kilimanjaro. Loan words in these languages indicate that the whole area had been settled earlier by Southern Cushites, who were only assimilated recently in the Taita Hills,[8] together with Southern Nilotic and Khoisan-speakers.

Farther north, Thagicu includes the Gikuyu, Meru, Kamba, and related languages of the central Kenya highlands. Thagicu is relatively homogeneous, indicating a split in their protocommunity late in the first millennium with subsequent differentiation of the languages over the following five hundred years. Ironworking sites in central Kenya date from early in the second millennium, leaving an unexplained gap of several hundred years between the development of ironworking and the Bantu languages in central Kenya and in the surrounding areas.[9]

The last relevant group of Bantu languages are the Northeast Coast Bantu (NECB) languages spoken today along the coastal lowlands and river valleys of southern Somalia, coastal Kenya, eastern Tanzania, and the Comoro Islands (see map 6). NECB is divided into four subgroups, implying that an ancestral protocommunity split initially into four before gradually expanding into the languages spoken today as outlined in figure 6. Though it is not clear how the initial protocommunity reached the east coast, it is likely that it was located somewhere in the area bounded by Mombasa and the Usambara, Taita, and Pare mountains.[10] Although there is not, and perhaps never will be, any direct evidence for this, it is implied by archaeological and linguistic reasoning. Within this area, two (Pare, Seuta) of the four members of the NECB are represented, and a third (Ruvu) adjoins it just to the south; on the basis of the theory of least moves, it is more economical to posit this as the NECB cradleland as it requires the movement of only one member (Sabaki) away. It is also here that we have the first example of the earliest east coast type of pottery assumed to be Bantu, Kwale ware, named after the second-century site at Kwale southeast of Mombasa. This date allows time for the breakup of proto-NECB into its four major groups and then into individual languages, one of which, Swahili, emerges into view in the ninth century, as we shall see.

The degree of lexical homogeneity between NECB languages is

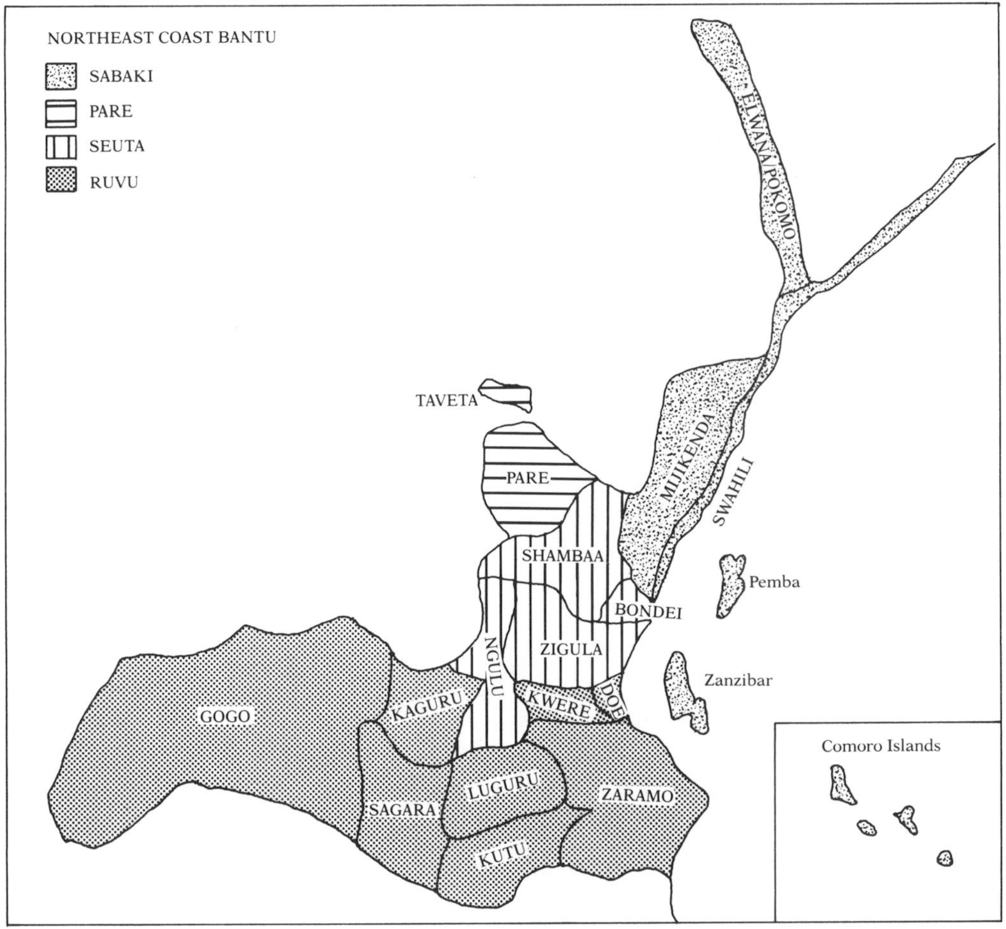

Map 6. Northeast Coast Bantu Languages

NORTHEAST COAST BANTU

- SABAKI
- PARE
- SEUTA
- RUVU

ELWANA/POKOMO

SWAHILI

MIJIKENDA

Pemba

Zanzibar

Comoro Islands

TAVETA

PARE

SHAMBAA

BONDEI

ZIGULA

DOE

KWERE

ZARAMO

NGULU

LUGURU

KUTU

KAGURU

SAGARA

GOGO

low, lower than Thagicu, Chaga-Taita, or Rufiji-Ruvuma, for example. Hitherto we have regarded lexical diversity as being primarily a sign of the early splitting of a protocommunity, but it can also result from geographical dispersal. When the members of a group are widely spread out, they are likely to come in contact with many other communities, which affect them in different ways and alter their vocabulary, resulting in a lack of lexical homogeneity. By contrast with Thagicu or Chaga, NECB languages are very dispersed, stretching from north central Tanzania along the Kenya coast to southern Somalia. Since this spread occurred from fifteen hundred years ago, the languages have had ample opportunity for modification.

One of the principal external modifying influences has been that of Southern Cushitic communities. We know from the presence of Southern Cushitic loan words in the NECB languages that in the past two millennia there have been Southern Cushitic communities in the areas inhabited by NECB and that contact did occur. Within the NECB homeland there were certainly early Southern Cushitic communities. More recently, individual NECB and Southern Cushitic communities jostled each other in their present locations. So we see a set of loan words that affected all NECB languages dating from the protoperiod, sets affecting the individual subgroups of NECB, and finally, sets particular to individual NECB languages. On top of these there is an overlay of Southern Cushitic loan words that have a broad areal distribution, the result of a general mixing of vocabulary and culture over the last two thousand years.

This is connected with our working assumption that when a practice or thing is transferred from one language to another the word for it is usually transferred at the same time. When such vocabulary refers to an aspect of culture or technology, it is likely to have been associated with the introduction of such an item. But replacement of vocabulary may take place at a time much later than the introduction of the objects or actions to which they refer. It is nevertheless an indication that the two languages concerned were in contact at some time. Taking Swahili in particular, we find most of its basic farming vocabulary derives from proto-Bantu, pointing to an unbroken tradition of more than three thousand years. Only a few crops such as *mtama*, "sorghum," and *mzuzu* (northern Swahili *izu*), "a type of banana," have infiltrated from Southern Cushitic languages, and since cognates for these have a wide distribution within Sabaki, NECB, and farther afield, they must derive from early NECB–Southern Cushitic contact in the first few centuries after Christ.

In the field of cattle husbandry, Southern Cushitic influence is more obvious. The proto-Bantu had small stock, and as we have seen, the eastern Bantu who emerged into East Africa acquired cattle and other stock although they did not represent an important element of the economy of many eastern Bantu subgroups. Swahili vocabulary again shows the same unbroken tradition, inherited from proto-Bantu. Words for items such as "calf," "sheep," "barren animal," "milk," "to churn" derive from Southern Cushitic. Most of them are not universal throughout the NECB languages but are mainly restricted to Sabaki, which suggests a slightly later contact, perhaps around the middle of the first millennium after Christ.

The Sabaki Languages and Swahili

The proto-NECB period did not last long. As the community broke up, the proto-Seuta and the proto-Pare hardly moved, while the proto-Ruvu slowly shifted south, eventually fanning out from around Dodoma to the Indian Ocean. The offshoot from which Swahili emerged, the proto-Sabaki, migrated north to the low-lying farming area marked by the Tana River in the south, the Indian Ocean in the east, and the plains along the Juba and Webi Shebelle rivers in the north.

As the proto-Sabaki moved north there was already some linguistic differentiation among them. Once a number of settled adjacent communities had been established, a sound change made at one point spread to others, as happens in any linguistic continuum. Other changes started at other points and spread, so that after some time the whole area was crisscrossed by lines of pronunciation (and other) differences. The major sound innovations within Sabaki indicate that in the homeland the ancestors of the Elwana and Swahili were adjacent, while those of the Comorians, Pokomo, and Mijikenda were also adjacent. At the same time, there are certain innovations shared by Comorian and the northern Swahili dialects (see Appendix 5), which imply that their ancestors lived side by side at one period. Gradually, over the centuries, one community after another moved south out of the northern homeland, taking their newly developed language features with them and allowing the remaining communities to interact in new ways.

When we ask where this homeland was, we choose a place from which subsequent migration could be explained by the least number of plausible moves. Of the five Sabaki languages spoken today, the two on the Tana River (Elwana, Pokomo) are within the bounds of the homeland area outlined above. All the northern dialects (Miini, Bajuni, Siu, Pate, Amu) of a third, Swahili, also lie within this area. The traditions of a fourth, Mijikenda, claim residence in the area as recently as four hundred years ago, as do those of many Pokomo and some Swahili communities (Bajuni, Jomvu, Kilindini, etc.). It is only the Comorian and the southern Swahili who do not recall unambiguous historical links with the northern coast.[11]

Such an explanation for a common origin in the north of all the Sabaki languages, including Swahili, is more economical and linguistically plausible than suggesting that parallel innovations developed by chance at different times and places. It also avoids the older fallacy that the various Swahili dialects sprang into life fully formed at different places along more than two thousand kilometers of coast. Rather than claim that as soon as any Bantu-speaking (or even non-Bantu-speaking) group touched the coast it automatically turned into Swahili under the influence of some unspecified force, it makes more sense to say Swahili dialects evolved in different places only after those places had been initially settled by Swahili-speaking migrants from a single area.

By looking at comparative vocabulary in today's languages, we can establish a reasonably detailed picture of the economy of the proto-Sabaki. It was strikingly similar in many ways to that of the proto-Bantu. They molded pots for cooking and storage. They smelted iron, although apart from weapon heads we have little clear idea of what they produced because of inadequate archaeological evidence. They hunted wild animals with trap and bow and arrow and exploited bees. They used canoes and fished in rivers and perhaps along the shore of the ocean, using line, net, and trap.

Domestic animals were numerous, including dogs, cats, chickens, goats, and sheep. The latter were an innovation probably deriving from Southern Cushitic influence. By A.D. 800 camels had been introduced by Eastern Cushitic migrants but never played a major role in proto-Sabaki society. Proto-Sabaki-speakers kept cattle, which they knew how to milk and bleed, but consideration of comparative vocabulary and of contemporary communities suggests that cattle keeping remained a secondary activity.

Essentially, they were subsistence farmers, with grains (sorghum, eleusine, millet, probably rice) and legumes (various identifiable beans and peas) central to their agriculture. They also produced sugarcane and ground fruits such as pumpkin/gourd and cucumber. Tree products were less important, the evidence pointing to castor

oil, wild dates, and certain types of palm. At a later stage they cultivated bananas and coconut, but we do not know when these were
introduced or how they spread. Hoes, machetes, axes, knives, mor-
tars and pestles, grindstones, and winnowing trays were used, and
there is a whole range of vocabulary associated with farming: to
cultivate, to plant, to dig, to harvest, to weed, to cut down, to pound,
to grind, to scrape, to winnow, to thresh, and chaff. Intoxicants were
probably brewed, grain was stored in raised granaries and at least
by the ninth century at some points on the coast, a kind of bread
was being baked in ovens.

Since the bulk of the population was concerned with farming
and the central part of their inheritance from proto-Bantu was agricultural, we can assume that the tradition continued unbroken
through proto-Sabaki times. The three river valleys in the region,
the Tana, the Juba, and the Webi Shebelle, were ideal for agriculture, and even parts of the coastal strip could have been used. An
oral tradition about the ancestors of the Pokomo and Mijikenda, the
Kitab al Zanuj, says that they "possessed cattle, sheep, and chickens,
and cultivated . . . beans and millet, but they had no fruit save that
of the bush." Various Arab writers between the tenth and twelfth
centuries also mentioned bananas, sugarcane, fruit, millet, and sorghum along the coast.

Some economic differentiation was present during the proto-
Sabaki period. Wild animal products could be supplied by the
proto-Sabaki themselves but also by Dahalo living north of the Tana
and by the earliest group of Eastern Cushites to reach the coast, the
Aweera. Hides and tusks were acquired by the proto-Sabaki, not just
for their own use but as barter items for ocean traders whose activities were recorded at least as early as the second century after
Christ in the *Periplus of the Erythraean Sea*, which describes the
bartering of imported for local goods in "market towns" along the
coast of Azania, a name covering the southern Kenyan and northern
Tanzanian coasts. Doubtless, in view of what we know of proto-
Sabaki vocabulary, there were villages on the coast where fish
formed a part of the regular diet. But it is not until the ninth century
that there is clear archaeological evidence for villages that were also
familiar with trading imported goods. Below later buildings made
of coral rag, the beginnings of the Swahili towns, there are the ruins
of fishing villages with mud and wattle structures and small quantities of imported pottery. These villages are located in two clusters
in the proto-Sabaki area, in open situations along the Somali coast,
adjacent to the farming settlements on the Webi Shebelle and the

Juba rivers, and on the islands of the Lamu Archipelago in northern Kenya where the harbors are better. It is to be emphasized that these signs of imported trade items are few. Local pottery far outweighs imported models at all sites along the coast. Early evidence for other imported goods is negligible until considerably later.

By the ninth century an early form of Swahili was probably spoken in these coastal settlements, not merely in the north but at least as far south as Kilwa. One of the methods used by historians for the early period in East Africa is to try to associate the geographical distribution of languages with the distribution of certain pottery types. We are able to say that certain early types of pottery, such as Urewe or Kwale ware, were associated with Bantu-speaking immigrants because they occur within the demonstrable Bantu-speaking area, because they are of a kind not previously present, and because they are associated with a cultural complex whose main elements are known to have been Bantu. In exactly the same way, we can correlate Swahili with early coastal sites. We know the location of all the towns and villages along the coast today where Swahili is spoken as the only language, and as far back as we have records they were Swahili-speaking. They are precisely the sites that had or have coral rag buildings and other archaeological evidence for a distinctive type of culture, including a distinctive type of pottery (Wenje ware). The coral rag trading towns themselves grew out of earlier mud and thatch fishing villages. Therefore we assume that at this time an early form of Swahili was associated with these villages. This is supported by traditions about who lived in the villages and towns scattered over two thousand kilometers of coast. The Swahili live in them now and claim always to have lived in them. Such Swahili literature as refers to them supports this claim. The few outside references we have support it. Conversely, no other single group along the entire coast, from Somali in the north or Makua in the south, claims to have built them, lived in them, or been associated with them. When peoples other than the Swahili were in them for any length of time, they decayed. When the Orma marched down the coast in the sixteenth and seventeenth centuries, the Swahili abandoned town after town, village after village, and the Orma did not live in them. In Somalia today the Old Towns are decaying or have decayed because the Somali do not maintain them or live in them. The Portuguese destroyed Kilwa and Mombasa, and the Swahili raised them up again.

There are also a small number of words cited by early Arab travelers that indicate that the inhabitants of the early towns were

Swahili-speaking. Some of these are Arabized names for items, some are undecipherable, some are so general in Bantu languages that they are not diagnostic, but a few make sense. Allowing for the possibility that the Arabic transcription may be inaccurately interpreted, we find *mufalume*, "chief" or "king" (al-Masudi, tenth century; modern Swahili *mfalme*), and *kundi/konde*, "a type of banana" (al-Idrisi, twelfth century; modern Swahili *ki-konde*). If we examine the distribution of these words in today's East African Bantu languages, we find they are limited to Swahili and a very few neighboring languages along the coast.[12] In most cases either the people who speak the neighboring languages are willing to admit that the words were borrowed from Swahili or there is linguistic reason to think so. This suggests strongly that the language for which these two words are quoted was an early form of Swahili.

This raises the question of the linguistic difference among Swahili, proto-Swahili, and proto-Sabaki and the related question of the cultural or economic differences among them. The answer to both is that there was no clear-cut distinction between the stages but rather a gradual transition. The proto-Swahili subsistence economy was not markedly different from that of other Bantu-speaking communities in East Africa at the time. It was only during the four centuries following the ninth century that the new elements that produced the Swahili way of life—ocean fishing, using oceangoing vessels, maritime trading, building coral and lime structures, urban settlements, Islam—were slowly added to the old. Only by the end of that period had they become an integrated way of life. Likewise, it is only linguists who superimpose ordered, labeled stages on the essentially organic development of languages. There never was a single point at which Swahili became clearly different from proto-Sabaki, and in the ninth century it would certainly have been more similar to neighboring Sabaki dialects than to modern Swahili. In this sense, there is little point in looking for a discrete Swahili presence before the ninth century.

Likewise, we cannot put an exact date on the proto-Sabaki or their settlement lands along the northern Kenya and southern Somalia coast. We have seen that by the second century after Christ Bantu-speaking immigrants had reached Kwale, near Mombasa, from the west or south. There is then an archaeologically unexplained gap until the ninth century, when we see the emergence of the earliest Swahili villages on the coast, from Somalia to at least southern Tanzania. But the coast itself was less favorable than the plains along the three northern rivers for an essentially agricultural population, and so presumably the proto-Sabaki lived inland and came down to the coast only occasionally to trade with outsiders and to fish. While ocean fishing was a considerable step from traditional river fishing, ocean fishing and trading with outsiders represented relatively minor activities and a later step from the preoccupations of most proto-Sabaki. We would therefore expect inland, riverside settlements to be somewhat earlier and might be justified in assuming a date in the middle of the first millennium after Christ for the advent of the agricultural proto-Sabaki in the northern homeland.

In summary, by A.D. 500 or slightly later, a Bantu-speaking population covered the area from the Tana River to the Webi Shebelle. They were essentially ironworking subsistence farmers and riverine fishermen based along the three main rivers and the limited stretches of coast suitable for agriculture. Hunting, stock keeping, ocean fishing, and trading with outsiders were minor activities. At this early stage it is not possible to correlate specialized economic activity with the particular ancestors of any of the later identifiable members of Sabaki, apart from noting that it was the Swahili and the Comorians who eventually took the large step from a land- to a sea-based economy and that both had started to move south by ship by the ninth or tenth century, the earliest dates for settlements in the south. As would be expected in a loose community stretched over some eight hundred kilometers, dialects existed among the proto-Sabaki community. During the second half of the first millennium after Christ this general situation continued, with some internal movement and slowly increasing economic and linguistic differentiation. Toward the end of this period we see clearer evidence of economic specialization and the first stages of a Swahili diaspora taking place.

3 THE EMERGENCE OF THE SWAHILI-SPEAKING PEOPLES

The specialization of the Sabaki-speaking communities and their dispersal from the northern homeland took place gradually over a period of seven centuries as distinctions began to appear among peoples widely dispersed within the homeland itself and were then accentuated as some groups started to move away. The earliest economic and social differentiation appeared as proto-Swahili- and proto-Comorian-speakers shifted to the coast and began to adapt to a maritime way of life. By the ninth century both lived on the coast and were sailing 800–1,000 km south to establish settlements along the Tanzanian coast and in the Comoro Islands. From the tenth to twelfth centuries further dispersion of Swahili-speakers from the homeland took place, north along the Somali coast as far as Muqdisho and south beyond Mombasa, while people continued to migrate from the homeland to Tanzania and new settlements were established as far south as Mozambique. By the twelfth century all the major Swahili towns of the coast had been established, but small-scale migrations continued as smaller towns and outlying villages rose and fell and individual Swahili traveled and migrated up and down the length of the coast. Meanwhile, in the northern homeland, early Mijikenda- and Pokomo-speakers remained living and farming along the river valleys of Somalia until the sixteenth century, when Orma pastoralists began to displace them and drive them south, the Pokomo settling alongside the Elwana on the Tana River while the Mijikenda moved on south to settle behind the southern Kenya coast.

With the movement of the Pokomo and Mijikenda, the present distribution of the Sabaki-speaking peoples was completed. The Sabaki languages spoken today are:

- Elwana: Also known as Malankote, spoken by riverine farmers on the upper Tana River between Rhoka and Garissa
- Swahili: Widely spoken by farmers, fishermen, and townspeople on the coastal strip and islands from Barawa to northern Mozambique (and, as modern Standard Swahili, throughout East Africa)
- Comorian: Spoken by fishermen and farmers in the Comoro Islands, each of the four islands having its own dialect
- Pokomo: Spoken by riverine farmers along the Tana River from its mouth upriver two hundred kilometers to Rhoka; subdivided into several dialects, the most significant distinction being between Lower and Upper Pokomo dialects
- Mijikenda: Spoken by farmers on the ridge just inland from the Kenya-Tanzania coast, from north of Malindi to Tanga; subdivided into ten regional dialects, the most important split being between southern (Digo, Segeju) and northern Mijikenda

Historically, these languages can be grouped into two basic subgroups of Sabaki—Elwana and Swahili on the one hand and Comorian, Pokomo, and Mijikenda on the other—on the basis of sound changes that occurred in their development (see Appendix 1), as represented in figure 7.[1] The basic split between Swahili/Elwana and the rest occurred early as a result of a south-north division within the homeland itself. Elwana today live along the Tana River and, according to their traditions, have always done so. The communities speaking the northern dialects of Swahili, one of the two major sections of Swahili, live in the region along the coast from the mouth of the Tana to north of the Somali border and also claim to have always lived in this area. Some southern Swahili traditions recall this area as their original homeland as well, and it is there where the greatest number of early Swahili settlements dating from the ninth century have been found. The early development of the Swahili peoples in this area will be detailed later; what is significant at this point is that both Elwana-speakers and Swahili-speakers were located initially at the southern end of the Sabaki spectrum. Early Comorian, Mijikenda, and Pokomo,[2] by contrast, were probably settled farther north along the Webi Shebelle and Juba river valleys and south as far as Bur Gao. The earliest Mijikenda traditions recall

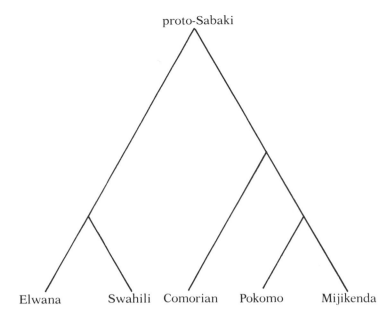

Fig. 7. Sabaki Languages

that they once lived as far north as Barawa and Muqdisho, where Mijikenda place names[3] and the presence of Kwale ware pottery attest to early Bantu-speaking settlements. Subsequently, they recall moving south to the Juba valley and the legendary Shungwaya, located somewhere along the southern Somali coast, before being driven farther south by Orma in the sixteenth century to settle in their present area behind the Kenya and northern Tanzania coasts.[4] Many Pokomo also recall living previously in Shungwaya and migrating south to the Tana River valley where they settled among Elwana-speakers, absorbing them or forcing them to move farther up the river. Comorians have no traditions relating to the northern homeland, but the relationship of their language to the other Sabaki languages, especially early Mijikenda-Pokomo, together with evidence that Comorian and Swahili, especially the northern dialects of Swahili, interacted while still in the homeland, indicates that they were probably located in between Mijikenda-Pokomo to the north and Swahili-Elwana in the south.

The divisions between the early Sabaki-speakers were not sim-

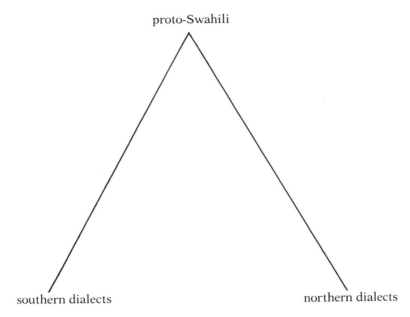

Fig. 8. Dialects of Swahili

ply geographical, however. While other Sabaki continued to farm along the fertile river valleys of the north, proto-Swahili- and Comorian-speakers moved to the coast and nearby offshore islands and began to adopt a maritime way of life. The settlements at Manda and Shanga show that they were already settled on islands in the Lamu Archipelago in small mud and wattle fishing and farming villages producing iron and Wenje-style pottery from early in the ninth century, but related settlements extending up the Tana as far as Wenje were still inland-based.[5] Contemporary with these was the settlement in the south at Kilwa, characterized by the same activities. Some Swahili were already traveling long distances by sea. With this and subsequent moves to the south, Swahili began to divide into its constituent dialects today. The initial split was between two dialect clusters, a northern one and a southern one, as shown in figure 8. The split between these two must have occurred early in the development of Swahili because of the relative antiquity of changes in sound and verb systems that have occurred subsequently in each (see Appendix 2).

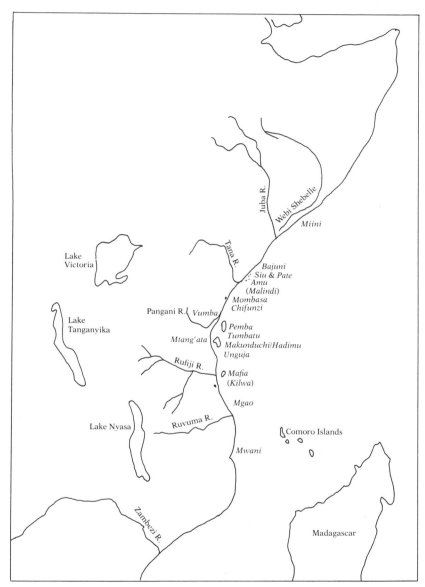

Lake
Victoria

Lake
Tanganyika

Juba R.

Webi Shebelle

Miini

Tana R.

Bajuni
Siu & Pate
Amu
(Malindi)
Mombasa
Chifunzi

Pangani R. *Vumba*

Pemba
Tumbatu
Makunduchi/Hadimu
Unguja

Mtang'ata

Rufiji R.

Mafia
(Kilwa)

Mgao

Lake Nyasa

Ruvuma R.

Comoro Islands

Mwani

Zambezi R.

Madagascar

Pemba = Swahili dialect

Map 7. Swahili Dialects in the Nineteenth Century

Northern Dialects of Swahili

The northern dialects of Swahili today include the following:

- Miini: Spoken at Barawa by two to three thousand people; may also have been spoken previously in Munghia, Merka, and Muqdisho
- Bajuni: Also known as Gunya or T'ik'uu, spoken from Kismayu south to just north of the Tana River at Mkokotoni along the mainland and adjacent islands, including some of those in the Lamu Archipelago; fifteen to twenty thousand speakers
- Siu: Spoken on Pate Island by six to seven thousand people
- Pate: Spoken on Pate Island; two to three thousand speakers
- Amu: Spoken on Lamu Island and adjacent mainland to the south; fifteen to twenty thousand speakers
- (Malindi): Mixed dialect based on Amu, resulting from repopulation in the nineteenth century; may have been a distinct dialect prior to the abandonment of Malindi in the late sixteenth century
- Mombasa: A series of subdialects spoken from Kilifi to Gazi, including Mvita, Jomvu, Kilindini, etc.
- Chifunzi: Spoken from Gazi to Wasin in southern Kenya by one to two thousand people

The northern dialects are distinguished from the southern dialects and from other members of Sabaki by having collectively undergone certain sound and grammatical changes. Since the Mombasa dialects and Chifunzi share only the two earliest of these (see Appendix 3a), their ancestors must have been the first to separate from the early northern dialect community. The next major division is between Miini and the remaining northern dialects; Miini does not show the innovations undergone by the others subsequently (see Appendix 3b), and it also retains a number of archaic northern features, as would be expected of such an isolated community. Differences among the remaining northern dialects—Bajuni, Siu, Pate, and Amu—are small, the main distinction being between Bajuni and the others (see Appendix 3c). We can thus represent the development of the northern dialects as in figure 9. Given that the greatest concentration of the northern dialects and differentiation is within the Lamu Archipelago and adjacent mainland, this was probably the ancestral homeland for the group as a whole. Mombasa-Chifunzi-speakers would have been the first to leave, moving south down the

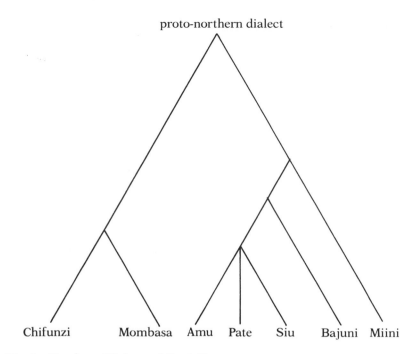

proto-northern dialect

Chifunzi   Mombasa   Amu   Pate   Siu   Bajuni   Miini

Fig. 9. Northern Dialects of Swahili

Kenya coast to settle at Mombasa and the south coast, followed by Miini-speakers moving north to Barawa and, some time later, Bajuni-speakers moving north along the islands of the northern Kenya and southern Somali coast, while Amu-, Pate-, and Siu-speakers remained in the archipelago.

This linguistic reconstruction of the early development of the northern dialects of Swahili in the Kenya-Somali coastlands compares favorably with other evidence for this area. The oldest coastal settlements yet discovered are Manda, Pate, and Shanga, all in the archipelago and dated to the ninth century. Mombasa was founded along similar lines ca. 1000, and a collection of similar sites is found along the Somali coast between Barawa and Muqdisho dated to the eleventh or twelfth century. A final series of sites, dating to the thirteenth and fourteenth centuries, is located along the coast and Bajuni islands from Lamu north to Kismayu.[6]

Although there is no direct evidence that these early communities were indeed Swahili-speaking, there are a number of grounds for connecting them with the early development of Swahili. Battuta noted in 1331 that Muqdisho had its own dialect, which was not Arabic, and referred to the coast midway between Muqdisho and Mombasa as "Swahilini," the land of the Swahili. Not only is this the first mention of the term; it also identifies the Tana-Lamu area as the central Swahili area. All the early sites are remarkably similar, characterized by farming, fishing, ironworking, and Wenje pottery, and all show a clear continuity in their subsequent evolution, indicating that they have been occupied continuously by Swahili-speaking peoples. Finally, old place names along the Kenya and Somali coast are Swahili, including many between Muqdisho and Barawa and sections within the old town of Muqdisho (such as Shangani) itself. Except for the small Miini-speaking population in Barawa, none of this area is Swahili-speaking today; these names must have been given by an earlier Swahili-speaking population.

If these early sites were inhabited by Swahili-speakers, then, the dating and sequence of their initial settlements accord well with the linguistic data, placing the beginnings of the northern dialect community in the early 800s in the Lamu Archipelago and lower Tana valley and the emigration of Mombasans in ca. 1000, Miini-speakers in ca. 1100, and Bajuni in ca. 1300. Given that Sabaki-speakers probably arrived in the northern homeland around the middle of the first millennium after Christ, the pattern of language development proceeded fairly rapidly, as was appropriate for a language community spread thinly over such a long distance. By 800 Swahili had emerged as a separate language and was beginning already to develop into distinct northern and southern variations. By 1000 the northern dialect itself had begun to split with the emigration of northern dialect-speakers to Mombasa, and it continued to do so with subsequent immigrations to Barawa and Muqdisho a century later and to the Bajuni islands two centuries after that.

Following these movements, each of the dialects became subject to separate influences. In the north Miini was influenced initially by neighboring Mijikenda-Pokomo-speakers[7] and subsequently heavily by Arabic, less so by Somali and Bajuni. Bajuni-speakers also influenced Siu and Pate. Bajuni traditions explicitly affirm that they occupied the coast from Kismayu south to Lamu prior to being driven south by Orma and settling in the Lamu Archipelago in the sixteenth and seventeenth centuries. Bajuni itself was influenced by its neighbors on the mainland, Dahalo and Aweera and Somali,[8] as

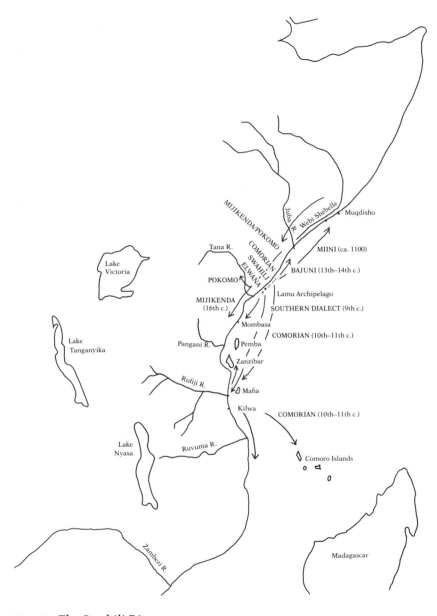

Map 8. The Swahili Diaspora

were Siu, Pate, and Amu to a lesser extent. More recently, Lamu became the main center of power within the archipelago as a whole, with the resultant influence of Amu on the other dialects and the spread of Amu along the adjacent mainland to the mouth of the Tana. Mombasa also became a major regional power and an influence on adjacent dialects, but the dialects of the southern Kenya coast also show some influence from the southern dialects of Swahili, which had been developing farther along the coast.

Southern Dialects of Swahili

The linguistic situation of the southern dialects today is confused by the high degree of bilingualism and bidialectism along the southern coast and the dramatic inroads made first by Unguja and then by Standard Swahili on local dialects over the last two centuries. In Mozambique, for example, most Swahili-speakers are bilingual in Swahili and Makua or Makonde, two local languages; whatever dialect was formerly spoken in Kilwa, the oldest known settlement in the south, has now been entirely replaced by Unguja; and in Tanzania nearly all coastal people now speak Standard Swahili either alone or in addition to their local dialects. Standard Swahili is based on Unguja, the dialect of Zanzibar Town, which was established on the mainland as the lingua franca of trade in the nineteenth century and was subsequently adopted by missionaries, by the colonial regimes, and as Standard Swahili by the independent government of Tanzania. In the process it has pushed back the rural dialects of Zanzibar, Pemba, and Mafia and flooded the opposite mainland, so reducing the extent and status of many local dialects that on a recent field trip along the northern Tanzania coast we were unable to find a single person who spoke pure dialect. Nevertheless, it is still possible to identify at least ten distinct southern dialects of Swahili.[9]

- Vumba: Spoken astride the Kenya-Tanzania border; formerly spoken on the islands and mainland to just north of Tanga
- Mtang'ata: Spoken along a twenty-kilometer stretch south of Tanga; probably spoken formerly from Tanga to just south of Dar es Salaam (see Lugha ya Zamani, below)
- "Lugha ya Zamani":   Formerly spoken just north of Tanga and south of Mtang'ata to just south of Dar es Salaam; essentially the same as Mtang'ata
- Pemba: Number of subdialects spoken on Pemba Island

- Tumbatu: Spoken on Tumbatu Island and northern Zanzibar Island
- Hadimu: Dialect spoken on southeastern Zanzibar Island
- Makunduchi: Dialect spoken on southeastern Zanzibar Island
- Unguja: Formerly spoken only at Zanzibar Town; expanded in the nineteenth century into Zanzibar, Pemba, Mafia, northern Madagascar, and the mainland opposite, including Kilwa (basis for modern Standard Swahili now widely spoken throughout East Africa)
- Mafia: Spoken on northern Mafia Island today; formerly spoken also in the southern part of the island
- Mgao: Spoken from south of Kilwa into northern Mozambique
- Mwani: Cluster of subdialects spoken on the northern coast and islands of Mozambique; sixty to seventy thousand speakers

Within the southern dialects there was an initial distinction between Mwani (probably with Mgao) and the others.[10] This was followed by an early split between Vumba and Makunduchi (Jambiani subdialect) on the one hand and the dialects centered on Pemba, Zanzibar, and the adjacent mainland on the other (see Appendix 4), with subsequent minor differentiation, as in figure 10.

The distinction between Mwani-Mgao and the others farther north suggests that the earliest settlement may have been at an intermediate location, such as Kilwa.[11] The prominence of Kilwa is indicated by the most recent archaeological work on the Tanzanian coast. Later settlements were established in the Vumba-Mtang'ata area and on Pemba-Zanzibar. Finally, communities fanned out throughout Pemba, northern and western Zanzibar, across the other islands, and along the coast from the Kenya border to south of Dar es Salaam. The high level of similarity between these dialects and the long undifferentiated stretch of coast where Mtang'ata[12] is spoken imply much mutual contact and a relatively recent and rapid spread of these dialects along the mainland coast. The overall picture, then, is more of a general dispersal from Kilwa than a staged or sequenced series of moves, such as occurred in the north. But this picture may be deceptive. Compared to the northern dialects of Swahili, the southern dialects have been phonologically very conservative, innovating little, either collectively or separately, since they left the northern homeland. Most of the differentiation that has occurred among them has been the result not of genetic develop-

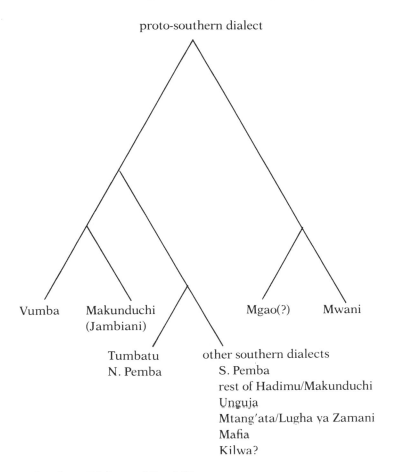

proto-southern dialect

Vumba   Makunduchi   Mgao(?)   Mwani
         (Jambiani)

Tumbatu   other southern dialects
N. Pemba   S. Pemba
                  rest of Hadimu/Makunduchi
                  Unguja
                  Mtang'ata/Lugha ya Zamani
                  Mafia
                  Kilwa?

Fig. 10. Southern Dialects of Swahili

ments but of the influences of other languages and dialects on them. Most southern dialects show considerable influence by northern dialects and Comorian, the result of a steady stream of additional migrants out of the north into established southern communities. Mombasa-speakers, for example, have influenced Vumba, Mtang'ata, and Pemba. Others have been influenced by mainland neighbors: Makua and Makonde have both exerted strong influence on Mwani; Seuta and Ruvu have influenced Vumba, Mtang'ata, Pemba, and the Zanzibar dialects; and Rufiji-Ruvuma has affected Mafia.

Unfortunately, this confusing picture is little clarified when we look at the other evidence pertaining to the southern Swahili. No systematic collection of oral traditions has been made for the Tanzanian coast, and no such material at all exists for the sizable Mwani community in Mozambique. Arab references to the Tanzanian coast and islands are uneven and ignore the Mozambique coast almost completely. Virtually no detailed archaeological work has been done on the northern Tanzanian coast or islands, thus precluding us from establishing these definitely as early settlement sites, and the extensive archaeological work by Chittick in the Kilwa area is of little help because we know nothing about what dialects were spoken there previously. Nevertheless, it is obvious that some southern dialect-speakers were present around Kilwa from early in the ninth century, where patterns of fishing, farming, ironworking, and Wenje pottery similar to those of the northern sites continued well into the eleventh century.[13] Kilwa thus seems to have been roughly contemporary with Manda and Shanga, but we can not be certain because the early dates in both areas rely on Islamic pottery types that span two centuries. So one might have been founded earlier in the period of this pottery's florescence than the other. Until more precise dating is done, however, we must conclude that southern-dialect-speakers left the northern homeland at an early date in the overall development of Swahili, establishing themselves initially at Kilwa by the ninth century. The choice of Kilwa is dictated by its having the earliest substantial archaeological site on the southern coast and by its traditions, which claim it was settled directly from the north. It was also adjacent to the trading network, which seems to have been centered on the southern Tanzanian coast during much of the first millennium.[14] The existence of this earlier network could have provided the impetus for the initial long move south from the Swahili homeland.

Subsequently, communities radiated out north and south from Kilwa along the coast and the islands of Tanzania and Mozambique. By the early fourteenth century Kilwa was prominent, but Zanzibar contained a number of thriving settlements by this time as well.[15] Earlier, al-Idrisi had mentioned both Zanzibar and Ngazija in the Comoro Islands as trade centers, noting that the people of the two places understood each other's language and included many Muslims.[16] Muslims were present on Zanzibar by A.D. 1107, the date of the earliest known mosque inscription, but not in Kilwa until the thirteenth century.

The case of Unguja is indicative of the mixed development of the southern dialects generally. Throughout coastal history there has been a constant stream of migration from north to south. We know this from oral traditions and the considerable number of northern dialect loan words in all the southern dialects. In general, southern dialect communities assimilated northern words as the northern immigrants who brought them were themselves assimilated to the southern communities they joined, losing their northern speech in the process. But the case of Unguja was different. The sound system and vocabulary of Unguja are basically those of the other southern dialects, with the usual addition of northern loan words. But the verb system of Unguja is different from that of the other southern dialects, having incorporated many of the elements typical of northern dialect verb systems, especially those of Lamu, Siu, and Pate.[17] Over time the Unguja-speaking community on the central western coast of Zanzibar must have received such a sustained influx of northern-dialect-speakers from the Lamu Archipelago that a number of structural features of the Unguja dialect itself were altered in the process. One other Sabaki language shows a very similar pattern of development, and that is Comorian.

Comorian

Though not a Swahili dialect, Comorian has often been considered to be one, and Comorian-speakers have a history very similar to, and intertwined with, that of the Swahili. Comorian speakers, like many Swahili, are island dwelling fishermen and farmers; Comorians have long been involved in Indian Ocean trade and share many historical traditions and processes with the Swahili; and Islam planted some of its earliest and deepest roots in the Comoro Islands. But Comorian is not Swahili, though its development has been linked with it in a number of different ways. Comorian is a Sabaki language and shares a number of features with the initial Pokomo-Mijikenda branch within Sabaki. While still in the northern homeland, however, Comorian-speakers interacted with Swahili-speakers, especially with the ancestors of the northern dialect community with whom they shared certain language innovations (see Appendix 5). Subsequently, Comorian also acquired a number of southern dialect features specific to Vumba and Makunduchi (see Appendix 4) together with others shared by all the southern dialects except Mwani (see Appendix 6). Comorian-speakers must therefore have migrated initially to the Vumba-speaking area, stayed there for some time to acquire these features, and then migrated to the Comoro Islands.

Comorian traditions claim that early Comorians came from Mrima, which usually refers to the northern Tanzanian coast, but Comorian use of the term to refer to all of the mainland coast is too ambiguous to be conclusive.[18] Idrisi discussed the Comoros in some detail, noting that the islands were heavily populated with dark people who traded with Zanzibar and understood the Zanzibari language. In 1154 Comorian and Zanzibar Swahili would have been easily intelligible with one another. By this time many Comorians were also Muslim and formed part of the same Indian Ocean trading world. Thus the Comorians must have passed down the southern coast sometime after the ninth-century establishment of southern dialect communities, but sometime before the twelfth-century account of Idrisi. Once established, Comorian itself began to develop into four regional dialects—Ngazija, Ndzwani, Mwali, and Maore—one on each island. The differentiation that occurred subsequently between these dialects is slightly greater than that between the northern and southern dialects of Swahili, but that is not unusual. Each dialect is particular to its own island, and the communities on each have developed to some extent separately from one another and from the Swahili-speaking mainland and islands 300 to 650 km distant. It is also probable that Malagasy-speakers occupied at least some of the islands prior to the Comorians and must have had some impact on the development of Comorian as they became absorbed into the new community. And over the last millennium all four dialects have absorbed loan material from Arabic, Persian, various Indian languages, both southern and northern dialects of Swahili, a number of mainland Bantu languages, and Malagasy, a dialect of which is still spoken in Maore today.

A Maritime Culture

Thus, by the fifteenth century, the Swahili-speaking peoples were widely scattered along the coast and nearby islands of eastern Africa, each settlement or local area having its own dialect of Swahili. Their spread had been rapid, especially in the ninth to twelfth centuries, and extensive. But once scattered, the peoples and dialects remained in close contact with one another, influencing each other's further development. The key to understanding these contradictory phenomena is the sea. Normally, we assume that languages expand slowly outward from a central core with a minimum of subsequent interaction. This is largely true for land-based languages, but the

Swahili became sailors, able to travel vast distances easily and rapidly, thus explaining how some of the earliest migrations extended over a thousand kilometers to the south and how widely scattered people continued to remain in close contact with one another thereafter. The traditions of Swahili towns and families are replete with the movements of small groups of people back and forth between the various settlements; most Swahili lineages today include members in a number of different towns; and individual Swahili traveled widely, visiting and residing in a number of different towns during their lifetimes. There has also been a continual north-to-south drift, fueled by the attractions of prosperous southern trading centers, repeated conflict among the northern towns, and the Orma and Somali invasions of the north in the sixteenth and seventeenth centuries. Thus, while the Swahili lived in widely scattered communities, each characterized by its own dialect, culture, and history, they also lived within a single larger community, knit together by their common language, their shared culture and history, and their mutual involvement in the Indian Ocean world. This contrast between the local and the wider community, between the particular history of individual towns and the general historical processes taking place the length of the coast, was to characterize the development of Swahili society from its earliest days.

4 EARLY SWAHILI SOCIETY, 800–1100

The earliest Swahili communities established as they scattered down the coast were small villages located on offshore islands or on the mainland foreshore. Their inhabitants fished, farmed, kept some livestock, and traded locally produced ironware, shell beads, cloth, and pottery with their mainland neighbors, but their harbors were generally not suited for extensive overseas commerce, and such trading was of secondary importance initially. We know all this from the locations of early settlements, from items found at the lowest levels of Shanga, Manda, and Kilwa dating from ca. 800 to ca. 1000, from words that all Swahili dialects share and that can be traced back to proto-Swahili, and from a few isolated references in early documentary accounts of the coast.[1]

The sea played a crucial role in early Swahili society, providing much of their livelihood and defining their distinctive development away from that of their Sabaki-speaking cousins. All Swahili settlements of this period were built on either beaches or small inlets close to the sea where small dugout canoes and sewn planked boats used for fishing within the reef or close to the shore could easily be pulled up on the beach. They fished for a wide variety of sea fish, using hooks and line, harpoons, nets, and basket traps. Shellfish and the occasional turtle, whale, or dugong were taken when available. All these items occur in the archaeological sites or in reconstructions of early Swahili vocabulary (see Appendix 7). They may have used seagoing outrigger canoes introduced earlier from southeast Asia along the southern coast as well, but in any case they learned to travel some distances on the open sea to fish and to reach such outlying islands as Zanzibar, Pemba, and the Comoros.

Though the sea increasingly came to define the Swahili, they also continued to farm. Swahili raised a variety of African crops, including sorghum, millet, eleusine, and rice, various kinds of peas, beans, and pumpkins, sugarcane, and castor oil, as well as coconuts, bananas, and taro introduced from southeast Asia. They cleared the bush with machetes and axes, cultivated and weeded with hoes, planted seeds with digging sticks, and harvested their crops, threshing and winnowing the grains to clean them and pounding them in a mortar with a pestle. They also raised chickens and some livestock—camels, cattle, goats, and sheep—milking and bleeding their animals, and hunted elephants and other wild animals using spears and poisoned arrows.

Each settlement was a compact village of mud and wattle houses surrounding a cattle kraal. The earliest houses were round, replaced later by rectangular ones, constructed by sinking poles vertically into the ground. These were then presumably joined by horizontal crosspieces, plastered with mud, and topped with a thatched roof, much as people continue to build today. Many settlements were later enclosed by walls, but in the earliest periods they were open to their fields, the surrounding bush, and their neighbors, with whom they must have enjoyed fairly amicable relations.

A main feature of these relations was trade. Swahili produced ironware, pottery, and shell beads for their own use and to trade with their neighbors. They smelted and forged their own iron, producing fishhooks, spearheads, and arrowheads, and perhaps axes and hoes. Along the coast they made their own pots in a single uniform style, termed "Wenje," indicating the degree to which these communities were all part of a single cultural complex. They may also have manufactured cotton cloth, though most of the evidence for this comes later, but they certainly ground shells in grooved blocks to produce beads to trade inland for ivory and skins. Their main overseas exports were ivory, slaves, ambergris, tortoiseshell, and leopard skins, for which they received Islamic pottery, glass vessels, and stone bowls in exchange. Though there were few imports in Kilwa and Shanga, by A.D. 1000 some 30 percent of the pottery at Manda was imported as it became one of the first villages to trade in a substantial way.

From that time trade increased everywhere along the coast, as indicated by greater quantities of imported pottery and glass trade beads. Cloth manufacturing had certainly begun, but iron remained the main item of trade with the peoples of the hinterland; Idrisi called it "the source of their greatest profits." With greater prosperity the number of settlements increased. By 1100 there were more than a dozen Swahili settlements between Munghia and Chibwene, but they remained small, rarely having more than a few hundred people each. More permanent houses began to be built, using squared coral blocks set in mud mortar as foundations for mud and wattle houses. This then was a period of economic expansion, but not one that appeared to cause substantial changes in Swahili social life.

This last statement is tentative because we know little of Swahili social organization, values, or beliefs during these three centuries. Masudi vaguely mentions the presence of rulers (*wafalume*), and his description of religion is equally enigmatic. After describing the people of the unidentified island of Kanbalu as "a mixed population of Muslims and Zanj idolators," he noted that the coastal peoples

have an elegant language and men to preach in it. One of their holy men will often gather a crowd and exhort his hearers to please God in their lives and to be obedient to him. He explains the punishments that follow upon disobedience, and reminds them of their ancestors and kings of old. These people have no religious law; their kings rule by custom and by political expedience. . . . Every man worships what he pleases, be it a plant, an animal, or a mineral.[2]

Such beliefs were clearly pre-Muslim, though with hints of Muslim overtones, but since we know of no mosques built anywhere along the coast before 1100, we must assume that the early Swahili were not Muslim. To learn more about their society and what they did believe, however, we must turn to their own traditions and the ways they recount the development of their societies in this period.

The Traditions of the Shirazi

Each Swahili town and family has its own traditions concerning its early development, but most begin with a tradition about the Shirazi.[3] A tradition collected in Kilwa is typical:

Of the original people who built Kisiwani, the first were of the Mtaka tribe, the second the people of Jasi from the Mranga tribe.
Then came Mrimba and his people. This Mrimba was of the Machinga tribe and he settled at Kisiwani. He became the headman of Kisiwani.

Then came Sultan Ali bin Selimani the Shirazi, that is, the Persian. He came with his ship, and brought his goods and his children. . . . They disembarked at Kilwa, . . . went to the headman of the country, the Elder Mrimba, and asked for a place in which to settle at Kisiwani. This they obtained. And they gave Mrimba presents of trade goods and beads.

Sultan Ali married Mrimba's daughter. He lived on good terms with the people. He gave them presents, each according to his standing. These presents were cloth and beads.

Then Sultan Ali persuaded Mrimba's daughter and said: "Tell your father, the Elder Mrimba, it is best for him to leave Kisiwani and live on the other side of the mainland. For it is not suitable for him to live in the same place as myself; . . . for he is my father-in-law. I will live here in Kisiwani; it will be enough if I manage our affairs. Whenever he wants to come to Kisiwani to see me, he can come, and likewise I can go and see him in the same way."

So Mrimba's daughter told her father what Sultan Ali had said. The Elder Mrimba agreed to what Sultan Ali wanted. But he said, . . . "Tell Sultan Ali, I am ready to go to the mainland, but he must spread out cloth for me all the way, so that I may walk on cloth as far as the mainland. I do not agree if it falls short." His daughter gave Sultan Ali his reply, as Mrimba had desired; and Sultan Ali agreed to Mrimba's wish.

So he spread out cloth from Kisiwani to the opposite mainland, and Mrimba passed over it thither. . . .

Then Sultan Ali ruled in Kisiwani. And Mrimba resolved to make war, and to come to Kisiwani and strike down Sultan Ali. So Sultan Ali had the Koran read out as a spell and offered sacrifices so that Mrimba should not take the road to cross over and bring war. Then Mrimba moved his home, and went to the mainland of the Ruvuma and dwelt there.

Sultan Ali only ruled the islands; he had no power on the mainland, but only the two islands, the first being Kisiwani, and the second Sanje ya Kati. He ruled in peace and with goodness towards the people, except that he made war on Sanje ya Kati. The work of the people was fishing and farming, and if they had other work from which they made a profit, we do not know about it. His subjects in these islands did not pay taxes. Sultan Ali did not build either a fort or a town wall. . . .

Sultan Ali had a child by Mrimba's daughter, a son, who was called Sultan Mohamed bin Sultan Ali. He lived at home until he reached manhood, and then set off and went to the Ruvuma to see his grandfather, the Elder Mrimba. When he arrived, his grandfather handed over his power to him, his grandson. So Sultan Mahomed [sic] ruled.

Then he gave him all the munitions of war and permission to make war on the mainland, first on Tungi, and then as far as Pemba ya Mnazi. Then he returned and came to Kisiwani. And, on the very day he arrived, his father Sultan Ali died.

So Sultan Mahomed ruled, because the people saw he had power on the mainland. His relatives, who had come from Shiraz, did not take power. And the people of the town followed Sultan Mahomed on account of his power.[4]

Other versions of the same tradition differ in detail, identifying the first Shirazi as Ali b. Husain and the local people as the Muli. Here Ali sailed down the coast with his father and six brothers in seven ships, each stopping to found a different town along the way. Ali stopped at Kilwa, gave gifts to the Muli, and persuaded them to move to the mainland, whereupon he dug out the channel between them so that when the Muli sought to return they were unable to cross back onto the island.[5] But all the versions have the same essential themes, summed up with brutal frankness by Burton, citing yet another version:

A certain Shaykh Yusuf from Shangaya [Shungwaya] bought land from Napendu, the heathen headman, by spreading it over with cloth, built the old fort, won the savage's daughter, slew his father-in-law, and became the sire of a long race of Shirazi "Kings of the Zinj."[6]

Settlers arrived; gave gifts to the local inhabitants to gain the right to settle on the island; consolidated that right through magic, deception, or might; and married local women whose children became dominant in Kilwa life.

These same themes recur frequently in the traditions of other Swahili towns. In the Lamu Archipelago, the people of Pate recall:

The origin of Pate was a person from the mainland whose name was Mwana Masuru who was of the Sanye tribe. Then there came a Batawi to trade and buy ivory from Masuru. He subsequently married Mwana Masuru's daughter, and so acquired possession of Pate. Then came the Nabahanis, Sefu and Sulaiman; Sefu married the daughter of Batawi. Seven days after the wedding Sefu went to his father-in-law to ask for his *fungoe* [dowry], and was given Pate.[7]

Another version states:

[Suleiman] remained in Pate with his people for he arrived with many men and ships and much wealth. Presently they sent gifts to the chief of Pate and to every big man in Pate they made a present, and even to the small men of the town they gave goods. Then the people, both great and small, perceived the goodness of the Sultan who had come from Maskat.

After he went to Is-hak, the chief of Pate, and asked for his daughter in marriage, and Is-hak gave him his daughter [called 'I Batawina] and he married her, and he rested with her the seven days of the honeymoon.

On the seventh day he came forth and went to see his father-in-law.

When he came Is-hak said to him "Your marriage portion is the kingdom of Pate."

So Suleiman ruled, and he had a son by that woman and he called him Muhammad.

Till in the year 625 Suleiman bin Suleiman died, and his son Muhammad bin Suleiman ruled and took possession of all his people, his wealth and his soldiers. It was he who first took the name of Sultan of Pate, and this by right, for his father came forth from their country bearing the title of Sultan.

The people of Pate loved him much for his own goodness, and because he was a child of the town, for his mother was of their kin.[8]

Here we see a succession of newcomers, each establishing themselves in the same way. The Batawi married the daughter of a local Sanye (Dahalo or Aweera) hunter, a woman, and acquired possession of Pate, while the Nabahani married the daughter of the Batawi and received Pate as her dowry, their son ruling as the heir to both lines.

In Lamu, traditions relate, the original inhabitants lived at Weyuni, just north of Lamu Town today, while immigrant Arabs from Syria settled to the south at Hedabu. Eventually the two fought, and the newcomers deceived the people of Weyuni into laying down their arms and slew them. The people of Hedabu became the Yumbe, People of the Palace, while the people of Weyuni became the Wayunbili, inferior people who were prohibited from making defenses or wearing footgear and were ordered to wash the bodies of the dead.[9] The Lamu chronicle thus provides a variation of the theme of integration, emphasizing violent conquest over peaceful intermarriage.

The traditions of Mombasa recall the original ruler as Mwana Mkisi, another woman, and the Shirazi as Shehe Mvita.[10] In Vumba the Shirazi are remembered as establishing Vumba Kuu and the eight Shirazi towns to the north, while on Tumbatu Island off Zanzibar, the first Shirazi married a local woman to give rise to the Tumbatu people.[11] Similar Shirazi traditions can be found elsewhere along the Mrima coast of northern Tanzania and on Pemba, Mafia, and the Comoro Islands. All portray similar patterns of immigration, interaction, and integration, with the Shirazi or their offspring emerging as dominant. Although the themes that run through these traditions are similar, it is not at all clear what they mean. Was the coast really conquered or settled by people from Shiraz? What is the significance of the common patterns of gift giving, marriages, and creation of new ruling dynasties that are portrayed?

Who Were the Shirazi?

Though Indian Ocean trade from the eighth through the eleventh centuries was largely dominated by Shiraz through the port of Siraf on the Persian Gulf, most of the actual boats and sailors trading to East Africa from the Gulf were Arab. During the eleventh century the center for Indian Ocean trade was changing to southern Arabia and the Red Sea, and by the twelfth century, when mosques began to appear along the coast and building in coral began, both of which traditions ascribe to the Shirazi, Shiraz was no longer significant in East African trade. It is unlikely therefore that the East African Shirazi came from Persia. This is confirmed by the paucity of Persian loan words in Swahili and the general lack of Persian inscriptions on mosques and tombs along the coast.[12]

A few of the traditions trace the Shirazi to Arabs from Oman, Muscat, or Syria, but the evidence for Arab influence along the coast before 1100 is also slight. There were few Arabic loan words taken into Swahili at this time, and coastal people were not yet Muslim. Who then were these mysterious Shirazi; where did they come from; and what do the stories about them mean?

A clue comes from frequent references in the traditions to Shungwaya, the legendary homeland of other Sabaki-speaking peoples in southern Somalia. The Bajuni of the Somalia-Kenya borderlands claim that their *waungwana*—the Ten Clans—came from Shungwaya, and each of these clans bears the name of a town along that coast.[13] The other Bajuni clans—the Eight—derive from people among whom they settled, and most have Somali names. Shirazi clans of Mombasa that date back to the time of Shehe Mvita—the Mvita, Jomvu, Kilindini, and Changamwe—also claim Shungwaya origins, as do Shirazi of Vumba, the Mrima, and Kilwa.[14] Other clans trace their origins from other towns farther north along the coast as people from the northern homelands continued to drift south to settle in the frequently more prosperous southern towns.

Those who claimed to be Shirazi were thus apparently coming from areas within the northern homeland. Even those whose ancestors may have come originally from the Middle East must have settled in this area initially, as some traditions claim, for most of those who moved south already spoke Swahili and were integrated into Swahili families and society. The term "Shirazi" has often been used to designate the historical Swahili as opposed to others who settled voluntarily or were forcibly settled as slaves on the coast during the nineteenth and twentieth centuries. Shirazi are the *waungwana,* old Swahili as opposed to new Swahili. To be Shirazi is to be a "real Swahili," a child of the motherland of Swahili language and culture. Throughout Swahili history there has been considerable movement between coastal towns, and most families can be found in more than one town. As one town became prosperous, other Swahili gravitated toward it. The Shirazi migrations were thus prototypical of recurring processes of movement, interaction, and integration that were to continue throughout coastal history.

If the Shirazi were prototypical Swahili, to what can we ascribe the name "Shirazi" with its clear reference to Persian origins? To understand this we must understand the politics of genealogies in African and Arab societies. In both, membership in a social group and one's status within that group were influenced by kinship, and one's genealogy was one's proof of membership and status. Thus, when people were adopted into a group, they eventually changed their genealogy to reflect their new social identity. Arab names and genealogies also frequently contain a place name from which an ancestor came as a *nisba,* or family name, but this too could be changed to reflect more prestigious origins if desirable. Thus, after the demise of Shiraz and Siraf, people of the successor town of Fal adopted the *nisbas* al-Sirafi and al-Shirazi even though they were from neither city.[15] The situation in East Africa must have been similar, with Swahili adopting the *nisba* Shirazi, since many of the Arab traders with whom they dealt, some of whom settled along the coast, had come from Shiraz.

The Significance of the Shirazi in Swahili History

In the Kilwa tradition, quoted at length above, a number of propositions are made:

- Kilwa was inhabited by a group of people before the Shirazi arrived.
- These people hunted on the mainland.
- The Shirazi gave gifts and paid tribute of trade goods and beads to the hunters.

- The Shirazi were traders: they gave trade goods, beads, and cloth, common trade items in East African trade.
- A Shirazi male married the daughter of the local leader.
- Citing in-law avoidance, he persuaded the local people to leave.
- They agreed to leave only upon a substantial payment of cloth.
- The Shirazi ruled the island, no longer paying tribute to the original inhabitants.
- These people sought to return.
- The Shirazi invoked superior Muslim magic and made sacrifices to deter them from returning.
- The Shirazi were subsistence farmers and fishermen; they paid no taxes.
- Kilwa was a village with neither a fort nor town walls.
- A son was born of the Shirazi and Mrimba's daughter.
- The son, on reaching manhood, sought out his grandfather Mrimba on the mainland and was given his power over the people and the right to make war against them.
- The son returned to Kilwa, his father died, and he succeeded him as the first ruler of the island *and* the mainland. Those who had come from Shirazi did not rule.

When we analyze these propositions in terms of the meanings they have for the Swahili, they establish a basic model for the development of Swahili society. The inhabitants of the land were people who hunted on the mainland; hunting, the mainland, and bush were all seen as "primitive" by Swahili. The Swahili, by contrast, arrived by sea from "Shiraz," the most sophisticated place known to them at the time. But the Shirazi were traders and had to settle with the hunters to obtain the products of the interior that they needed. Furthermore, the Shirazi had to settle as clients because Mrimba's people had prior claim to be "owners of the land." The Shirazi were able to resolve this dilemma by marrying local women and taking advantage of their matrilineal links to obtain rights to settle, rights they sought to extend by citing rules of in-law avoidance and through purchasing the land outright by, literally, covering it with cloth. Though *waungwana* frequently held land in freehold, mainland peoples and poorer Swahili exercised use rights only over inalienable ancestral land, so Mrimba disputed the permanent alienation of the land of his maternal ancestors and sought to recover it by force. At this point the Shirazi invoked the superior ritual power of Islam, asserting for the first time a Muslim basis of Swahili society in contrast to the (assumed) ancestor veneration of the local inhabitants. This claim does not mean, however, that the first Swahili were Muslim at that time. Traditions are always told retrospectively, and Islam was to become one of the defining characteristics by which Swahili asserted their superiority over mainland peoples. The Swahili had yet to develop in other areas as well, continuing to live in a village without taxes, forts, or town walls, all features of the town-state of the future.

Potential conflict between two sets of forces—those of hunting, the land, the matrilineage, and the ancestors versus those of fishing and farming, the sea, the patrilineage, and Islam—was ultimately resolved in the single heir to both sets. The son of Ali and Mrimba's daughter inherited rights to the mainland matrilineally from his grandfather Mrimba and rights to power and status patrilineally from his father. The two lines were merged, and the legitimacy of the new people was established, a people who were neither local nor Shirazi, as the tradition carefully points out. This synthesis can still be seen on neighboring Mafia, which shared the same Shirazi dynasty, where *waungwana* Mbwera claim to be both "owners of the land" and Shirazi rulers as a result of intermarriage between the two.[16]

A similar point emerges from the Pate tradition. There the initial inhabitant was a Dahalo or Aweera hunter whose daughter married Batawi, the trader who had come for ivory and who stayed to take possession of the town from his wife and mother-in-law. The scenario was repeated when a Nabahani arrived, married the daughter of Batawi, and received the town as his dowry, their son becoming the first sultan "by right, for his father came forth from their country bearing the title Sultan . . . and because he was a child of the town, for his mother was of their kin." The three lines never became integrated as in Kilwa, however, but remained three distinctive strata within Pate society. Hunters continued to inhabit the mainland, and the people of Pate remained dependent on them as allies and as suppliers of ivory. The Batawi continued to exist as a prominent *waungwana* clan within Pate society. And the Nabahani ruled as a hereditary aristocracy. The tradition thus establishes a series of relationships between the different groups in the town in the hierarchical, stratified Swahili mode. Interaction between traders and local peoples could thus result in a variety of syntheses, each particular to a town and its historical circumstances, but all occurred within the common historical process delineated by the traditions of the Shirazi.

The traditions present indigenous models for the development of Swahili society, analogical statements that extract recurring elements from the diversity of historical experience to explain how Swahili society came to be. The roots of that society are seen in the interaction between indigenous peoples of the mainland and island traders who arrived as strangers, paid tribute to the local peoples, and made marriage alliances with them to gain rights in land but who ultimately were assimilated within a society that was simultaneously becoming economically differentiated and socially stratified. These themes reflect the tensions inherent within Swahili societies and represent the resolution through institutionalization of those tensions in a stratified model of coastal society, a society that came to embrace a wide range of economic groups and statuses. The symbolism of the traditions is of marriage and descent. Shirazi males married indigenous females; their sons inherited rights to land through their mothers and rights to status and wealth from their fathers. The use of the idiom of cognatic descent in the traditions uses the opposition and accommodation inherent in marriage to express the conflicting tensions between differentiation and assimilation. The Shirazi became a part of coastal society, but that society changed to become less homogeneous and less egalitarian. Within an expanding international economy, some became more wealthy than others. Within the common political unit of each town, some became more powerful. And within a common social structure, numerous subcultures appeared and acquired differential statuses within the whole.

At the same time, Swahili families retained their connections to their own and other families elsewhere on the coast through their common identity as Shirazi, a term that itself became a family name in a number of places. Kinship thus linked them both to the local community in which they lived and to the wider community of trade and coastal society in general. This pattern remained typical of the Swahili, as traders continued to take local wives to attain local economic and political connections and status while retaining their own kinship links to the wider coastal community to maintain the networks of trade and symbols of power. The Shirazi of the traditions were thus the bridge linking the old society with the new, the local with the world of the coast and the Indian Ocean beyond.

The traditions of the Shirazi relate directly to the formative period of coastal societies, for the period of Ali b. Husain of the Kilwa tradition has been dated to the end of the eleventh century.[17] Thus the Swahili were undergoing fundamental social changes during this period of their history, as maritime trade began to supplant subsistence production. Homogeneous fishing and farming villages were becoming heterogeneous towns as Swahili from elsewhere along the coast were attracted to new trading centers. Classes developed, each of which sought to entrench its position through appeals to prestigious origins, superior ritual power, and a more sophisticated culture. Classes became strata, each rooted in its own traditions and localized in its own lineages and wards of the town. Neither Islam nor kings had yet made their appearance in Swahili society, but the economic and social differentiation that had begun to occur before 1100 was to set the stage for further differentiation to come.

5   RISE OF THE SWAHILI TOWN-STATES, 1100–1500

Developments among the Swahili towns and villages along the coast occurred more rapidly as trade expanded from the twelfth to the fifteenth centuries. This is the period that gave rise to the great towns of Muqdisho, Lamu Malindi, Mombasa, and Kilwa before the combination of the Portuguese entrance into the Indian Ocean from the south and the Orma and Somali invasions of towns from the north brought a hiatus of two centuries in their continued development. Though the Portuguese were able to extract tribute on occasion and repeatedly sacked Kilwa and Mombasa during the course of the sixteenth century, they never were successful in ruling the coast, and they made almost no enduring impact on Swahili culture. What was more critical to the fate of the Swahili towns was that, in their attempt to monopolize the gold trade from Sofala and Kilwa, the Portuguese succeeded in destroying it altogether through destruction of the local infrastructure, overtaxation, and the provision of shoddy goods.[1] Individual towns reverted to local trade, and the gold trade became dispersed among small traders along the Mozambique coast. Not until the eighteenth century would the Swahili towns again be able to concentrate trade and wealth on the earlier scale. While the Portuguese were attacking the economic base of the Swahili towns in the south, Orma and Somali invasions of the northern coast, from the Juba to south of Mombasa, caused numerous northern settlements to be abandoned during the late 1500s and early 1600s. When the Swahili towns prospered again in the eighteenth and nineteenth centuries it was under the impetus of Omani-dominated trade and accompanied by markedly greater Arab influences. It was then that great numbers of Arabic loan words entered the Swahili language, architectural motifs began to imitate Arab ones, and coastal Islam was revitalized by immigrant *sharifs* from southern Arabia, giving a more Arabian tone to Swahili society. The fifteenth century thus represents a peak in the development of the Swahili towns as an indigenous form, the culmination of seven centuries of internal growth and historical development.

The evidence for the expansion of Swahili society during the twelfth and thirteenth centuries includes the earliest uses of coral for building and the first appearance of mosques, along with increasing quantities of Islamic and Chinese pottery and imported glass beads, while the florescence of Swahili culture in the fourteenth and fifteenth centuries is evidenced by extensive building in coral—houses, mosques, tombs, and palaces—accompanied by dramatic increases in imported trade goods. This can be seen from the ruins of towns such as Shanga, Mombasa, and Kilwa, but our picture of the towns during this period is made more vivid by the descriptions left by travelers who visited the coast during its peak. The first traveler to visit the coast and report on what he saw, Ibn Battuta, provides us with detailed accounts of Muqdisho, Mombasa, and Kilwa in 1331. Yaqut had reported a century before that Muqdisho was the most important town on the coast and that there were foreign Muslims in residence, but he also noted that the neighboring peoples were nomads, each clan having its own elders.[2] By the time of Battuta's visit, Muqdisho had grown to a large town where cotton trade cloth was made, whose merchants were wealthy, and whose ruler was a *sheik*, a wise and pious Muslim. Battuta discusscd points of religious law with the chief *qadi* and described in detail the procession of the *sheik* from the Friday mosque:

Over his head they carried a silk canopy, its four poles topped with a golden bird. He wore a sweeping cloak of green Jerusalem stuff, over clothes of Egyptian linen. He had a silk girdle and a large turban. In front of him they beat drums and played trumpets and oboes. He was preceeded by the amirs of the army, and followed by the Qadi, the lawyers and the Sharifs.

Later he had an audience with the ruler, flanked by officials. Soldiers drilled; drums, trumpets, and oboes played; and people petitioned the ruler, who referred questions of religious law to the *qadi* and other cases to the council.

Mombasa was not nearly so grand, but its people were sufficiently wealthy to import their food from the Lamu area, were Shafi'i Muslim, and attended wooden mosques. Kilwa, on the other hand, Battuta remarked,

is one of the most beautiful and well-constructed towns in the world. The whole of it is elegantly built [or, built of wood]. The roofs are built with mangrove poles. . . . The chief qualities are devotion and piety; they follow the Shafi'i rite.

Its people were black, and the sultan, Abu'l-Mawahib, was known for his learning, piety, humility, and charity.[3]

By the early 1500s when a number of Portuguese reported on their visits to the coast, the situation was even more impressive. Muqdisho was still "a large town, with houses of several stories, big palaces in its centre, and four towers around it,"[4] and Barawa to the south "was governed by a corporation, these twelve Moors being the principal heads of the government."[5] Farther down the coast, Lamu and Pate were towns of the "Moors," who traded inland, and were well walled with stone and mortar. Pate, though possessing a poor harbor, had an active commerce with southern Arabia, was "very large" and had "many fine edifices," was ruled by a king, and was the sole manufacturer of "very rich silk cloths, from which the Portuguese derive great profit in the other Moorish cities where they are not to be had."[6] Manda and Shanga had both reached their peak earlier, however, and were not mentioned by the Portuguese. Manda, a pre-Muslim town, witnessed extensive building from the early 1000s to the early 1200s before going into decline, while Shanga reached its peak from ca. 1320 to ca. 1440 with extensive building in coral rag and lime. By the beginning of the Portuguese period, both towns were in ruins, destroyed by the trade rivalries and intertown wars that plagued the Lamu area at that time.[7]

Malindi was prospering, however. Developed in the 1100s as an iron exporter,[8] by 1498 it was a town of lofty white houses whose

king wore a robe of damask trimmed with green satin, and a rich turban. He was seated on two cushioned chairs of bronze, beneath a round sunshade of crimson satin attached to a pole. . . . There were many players of anafils, and two trumpets of ivory, richly carved, and of the size of a man, which were blown from a hole in the side, and made sweet harmony with the anafils.[9]

Women with vases of incense flanked the entrance to the king's house, and the king rode over a sacrificial sheep for "enchantment."[10] And Mombasa had certainly grown since Battuta's time:

Mombasa is a very large town and lies on an island from one and a half to two leagues round. . . . The houses are of the same type as those of Kilwa; some of them are three storeyed and all are plastered with lime. The streets are very narrow, so that two people cannot walk abreast in them; all the houses have stone seats in front of them, which makes the streets even narrower. . . . The town has more than 600 houses which are thatched with palm leaves. . . . In between the stone dwelling-houses there are wooden houses with porches and stables for cattle. There are very few dwelling houses which have not these wooden houses attached.

Ships from India were in the harbor. "There was a large quantity of cotton cloth for Sofala in the town, for the whole coast gets its cotton cloth from here."[11] "It has its own king, himself a Moor. The men are in colour either tawny, black or white, and also their women go very bravely attired with many fine garments of silk and gold in abundance."[12] Stone building in Mombasa had begun about 1200, following an upsurge in trade and importation of pottery in the late 1100s, and continued through 1500.[13] When the Portuguese sacked the town in 1505, they found gold and silver, rich silk, gold-embroidered clothes and carpets in abundance; Mombasa had become the most important town on the Kenya-Somali coast.

Ironically, given their importance later in the eighteenth and nineteenth centuries, Zanzibar and Pemba were not often noted. Each island contained a number of towns and villages, the main towns on Zanzibar being Unguja Ukuu and Tumbatu. Both engaged in entrepôt trade with the mainland, trading ivory, gold, ambergris, and aromatic woods for cloth and imported pottery, and both appeared to be Muslim. The earliest dated mosque inscription on the eastern African coast at Kizimkazi had a *qibla* date of 1107. Documentary accounts all note that the townsmen were Muslim and that there were numerous mosques, but there were also large numbers of people in the interior of the islands who periodically raided the towns and presumably were not Muslim.

The kings of these isles live in great luxury; they are clad in very fine silk and cotton garments which they purchase at Mombasa from the Cambaya merchants. The women of these Moors go bravely decked, they wear many jewels of fine Cofala gold, silver too in plenty, earrings, necklaces, bangles, and bracelets, and they go clad in good silk garments.[14]

The general lack of material, both documentary and archaeological, on Zanzibar and Pemba is something of a mystery. During the tenth century ships sailed directly from the Gulf to Kanbalu, the most notable trade center off the coast. The site of Kanbalu has yet to be located, but it may have been on Pemba,[15] and extensive ruins exist at both Unguja Ukuu and Tumbatu. Yet for some reason few later travelers mentioned these towns, and the Portuguese, always with an eye to where the wealth was, largely ignored them. We can only conclude, therefore, that they were probably not significant centers of Swahili development.

There is certainly no doubt, however, about the prominence of Kilwa and its satellite Mafia. In 1500, it was noted that

The island is small, near the mainland, and is a beautiful country. The houses are high like those in Spain. In this land there are rich merchants, and there is much gold and silver and amber and musk and pearls. Those of the land wear clothes of fine cotton and silk and many fine things, and are black men.[16]

Two years later we learn that

The city is large and is of good buildings of stone and mortar with terraces, and the houses have much wood works. The city comes down to the shore and is entirely surrounded by a wall and towers, within which there may be 12,000 inhabitants. The country all round is very luxuriant with many trees and gardens. . . . The streets of the city are very narrow, as the houses are very high, of three and four stories, and one can run along the tops of them upon the terraces, as the houses are very close together; and in the port there were many ships.

A Moor ruled over this city, who did not possess more country than the city itself.[17]

The source of Kilwa's wealth and power was its control over the transshipment of gold from Zimbabwe through Sofala on the Mozambique coast to the Middle East and India from the early 1200s, initiating three centuries of growth. As trade boomed, Kilwa collected customs duties totaling six-sevenths of the cloth traded to Sofala plus 2 percent of the cloth's value in gold, or over 80 percent.[18]

Kilwa peaked well before the Portuguese arrival. From ca. 1150 to ca. 1300 there is considerable evidence for increasing wealth. Imported glass trade beads largely supplanted earlier local shell ones; imported pottery increased in quantity; and spindle whorls for cloth manufacturing increased. Three mosques were built on Mafia; building in stone using lime mortar began; and copper coins were minted in the name Ali bin Hasan late in the period. From ca. 1300 to ca. 1400 the tempo of building increased dramatically with the construction of the Great Mosque and Husuni Kubwa, a huge structure with a sunken courtyard, domes, vaults, and extensive carved-stone decorations. Local pottery also underwent a creative surge, and imports of fine pottery and glass beads increased. During the final period, ca. 1400 to ca. 1500, there was a slight decline in Kilwa's fortunes. Ironworking and cloth manufacturing ended as Kilwa completed the transition from a local manufacturing center to an international trading entrepôt, but large-scale building also ceased and there was a revival of local building styles. Kilwa had evidently become heavily dependent on trade, with the result that it rapidly declined to little more than a local village following the Portuguese disruption of the gold trade at Sofala.[19]

Wealth, Power, and Authority

A number of important changes thus occurred between 1100 and 1500 all along the coast: construction in stone began and reached impressive heights of artistic accomplishment; Islam began to spread down the coast, flourishing in the major trading centers of Muqdisho, Mombasa, and Kilwa; and rulers rose to power and were surrounded by elaborate courts. Much remained the same, however: local pottery predominated over imported varieties; most of the building in poorer towns and even in the midst of prosperous ones like Mombasa was in mud and wattle; and local trade in grains and locally produced cloth, iron, and beads continued to underpin international trade in ivory, ambergris, and gold. But, as trade expanded, an increasingly wealthy class of merchants grew up who, by restricting access to wealth, were able to monopolize political power. Though we lack the detailed evidence to know precisely how individual traders gained wealth and power or how specific towns were able to develop, expanding trade at different times and in various towns along the coast was generally followed by the development of more stratified societies and more hierarchical political structures as wealthy traders made propitious marriages, sponsored communal mosques and festivities, and generally developed extended networks of allies and clients who would support them in town politics. In some cases the ruling class took the form of oligarchies of wealthy *waungwana*, in others of small aristocracies of royalty.

Oligarchic republics developed initially in Muqdisho, Barawa, Lamu, Mombasa, the Shirazi towns of the Mrima coast, Tumbatu, Hadimu, and the Comoro Islands and remained the underlying political structure in many of these areas. In Muqdisho, Yaqut had reported ca. 1220 that each clan had its own elders, and a century later Battuta noted that elders continued to wield power within an elaborate court in which authority had become divided among a king, Muslim clerics, and the elders. Barawa was governed by a council of elders at least until 1500, and Lamu maintained such a system well into the nineteenth century, providing us with a modern example of oligarchic rule with which to compare earlier accounts.

Lamu society in the early nineteenth century included the prominent old families, or *waungwana,* who occupied the central wards while Swahili from other towns, poorer Swahili farmers, fishermen, and craftsmen, together with Arab traders and Dahalo and Aweera hunters, Pokomo farmers, and Orma herders and cattle traders, occupied the mud and thatch ones on the periphery. Each ward was formed around a few families who lived in close proximity to one another, attended the same mosque in their ward, intermarried, and worked together in common economic enterprises. One family or ward might monopolize a certain political or religious office or a branch of trade, but each was linked to other families and wards in the wider context of the town economy, town politics, and communal rituals.

Each individual also belonged to a named patrilineage, which was ranked vis-à-vis other lineages in much the same way as wards. Since members of lineages of comparable status tended to intermarry, certain lineages often became concentrated in certain wards, especially in the nine central *waungwana* wards. Each lineage also had its functional responsibilities. The result was a complex distribution of offices and responsibilities among different lineages and wards. Thus the Friday mosque was located in Pangahari ward in the Zena half of town, but the preacher came from the Maawi clan in the Suudi half. The annual ritual perambulation of the town started in Suudi, overseen by the Friday preacher, but ended in Zena with the ritual sacrifice of an ox. Political power was shared among the oldest wards and lineages, the three main *waungwana* lineages providing fifteen members of the council out of a total membership of twenty-two, and council leadership alternated every four years between the five *waungwana* wards of Zena and the four of Suudi.[20]

These practices stemmed from long-standing ideas held about the historical origins of different groups and about proper social behavior. *Waungwana* generally traced their origins to the earliest inhabitants of Lamu in oral traditions and in the genealogical book (*silwa*) maintained for this purpose, while individual families accounted for their particular town responsibilities by the historical roles played by their ancestors. *Waungwana* restricted their daughters from marrying social inferiors and adopted a genteel, urbane mode of dress and discourse. Such a system was not static; prominent families and wards could maintain their position only as long as they were able to retain economic and political power. el Zein has shown how immigrant Hadrami merchants and *sharifs* in the later nineteenth century were able to capitalize on their economic power, religious prestige, and the political leadership of the inhabitants of Suudi to counter *waungwana* ideology with a more egalitarian ideology based on the brotherhood of all believers. As intermarriage between the two groups increased and descent became confused, the *silwa* was symbolically thrown into the sea; and as Zena and Suudi became overpowered by fringe dwellers, the two coalesced into a single moiety, Mkomani, opposed to the newcomers in Langoni. Thus economic prosperity was a mixed blessing for the old Swahili families, bringing them wealth and power but also competition as immigrants from other towns and peoples flooded in and capitalized on new economic and political opportunities to promote their own status.[21] The position of a particular family or ward within the social structure of the town as a whole was thus a historical product, born out of the dynamic tensions inherent in Swahili economy and society and closely reflected in the history recalled by the people in their own oral traditions, thus revealing some of the historical processes underlying the development of the coastal towns generally. Not all towns developed in identical ways; we have evidence that each developed differently into a distinctive historical entity. But the detailed analysis of Lamu in the nineteenth century reveals many of the general processes common to the development of all as well as many of the representative institutions that emerged during their development. As a historical product, modern Lamu represents the culmination of many of the historical forces whose roots and development in earlier centuries are revealed in the traditions of the coast.

In Lamu these traditions continued to favor the *waungwana* families generally until the middle of the nineteenth century, but elsewhere along the coast the traditions recounted the exploits of royal families such as the Nabahani of Pate or the Shirazi and Mahdali of Kilwa. The establishment of the Shirazi presence at Kilwa came about through the marriage of Ali the Shirazi to Mrimba's daughter, as we have seen, resulting in the right of their son to rule as the child of both groups. The remainder of the tradition consists of a long recitation of the rulers who followed Ali and reveals how the concentration of political power came about.[22] Though the tradition ostensibly recounts a straightforward list of successors to the throne of Kilwa established by Ali, it also reveals that the process of centralization was achieved only slowly over more than a century (see fig. 11). Though Ali b. Husain (a/A) was noted for acquiring Kilwa, he actually died on Mafia, and three of the sons who succeeded him, Muhammed (b), Bashati (c), and Daud (d/C), also ruled on Mafia while a grandson, Ali b. Bashati (B), ruled on Kilwa. Ali b. Daud (D) succeeded his father, but he was driven to Mafia by a usurper, Khalid b. Bakr (E) from the island of Sanje ya Kati. The dynasty was then restored by another grandson of Ali, Hasan b. Sulaiman (F/H), but his reign was interrupted by another usurper, the *amir* Muhammad b. al-Husain (G), before he regained the throne and passed it to yet another grandson of Ali, Hasan b. Daud (I). Of the first ten rulers, then, seven were either sons or grandsons of Ali while two were usurpers, and many of the earlier ones spent much of their time on Mafia, indicating that the dynasty had in fact come from Mafia initially and took some time to establish itself on Kilwa. This initial centralizing period, dating from ca. 1100 to ca. 1200, coincided with the initial mud-and-wattle period at Kilwa, further indicating that these early rulers may have been no more than Shirazi traders from Mafia who slowly gained prominence on Kilwa in a period of increasing trade.

The remaining Shirazi rulers are all associated with the period of Kilwa's development when building in coral began. Daud b. Sulaiman (K) established the gold trade to Sofala; Sulaiman b. Hasan (L) was the first to build in stone; and Daud b. Hasan (M) and Ali b. Hasan (P) were the first to mint coins. Thus, by capturing the gold trade this Shirazi family was able to establish its undisputed authority over Kilwa, to begin the program of coral building, and just possibly to have recognized its ancestors retrospectively as kings, thus reinforcing its emerging authority with the claim to early settlement and legitimacy established by tracing the dynasty back to the Shirazi founder Ali b. Husain. Wealth thus led to the promotion of one family into power, which it then used to establish its legitimacy as the ruling authority over other *waungwana* families. The transition from oligarchy to royalty was complete, but the Shirazi family was not to retain this monopoly for long, as another nonroyal *amir*, Hasan b. Talut (1), seized the throne after the death of Ali b. Daud (R) and established a new dynasty.

Without going into the details of the individual successions and reigns, a number of important themes emerge from this new dynasty's history. The dynasty was established by a nonroyal *amir* who had served in the previous government. There was thus an essential continuity in the system and not the sharp discontinuity of a conquering immigrant dynasty postulated by Chittick to explain the rapid development of Kilwa from ca. 1300. What had changed were the personnel in authority, not the nature of authority itself. The power of nonroyals had been demonstrated by two usurpations by *amirs* during the Shirazi period and was to be reasserted during the second half of the Mahdali dynasty when a series of powerful *amirs* dominated politics, determining successors to the throne, unseating them once there, and in one case, appointing a nonroyal, Hasan b. Sulaiman (24/26). Their leverage came partly from the proliferating number of royals and the inevitable factionalization of the politics of succession that this brought about. But it also came from the continuing power of officials and from the declining wealth of monarchs who were easily dominated by wealthy *amirs*. Both nonroyal *amir* usurpers, Muhammad b. Sulaiman (16) and Muhammad Rukn al-Din (31), were noted for their great wealth and generosity. Power apparently continued to be split between Kilwa and Mafia. The new dynasty was not legitimated until Abu'l-Mawahib (4), after whom it was named. While this process of legitimation was going on, Shirazi continued to rule at Mafia, and the Mahdali dynasty itself subsequently split between the two and was not reunited until Muhammad al-'Adil (13). Kilwa politics frequently spilled out of Kilwa as losing factions emigrated and established their own settlements elsewhere. Hasan b. Sulaiman (24/26) established his own successful town on the mainland after he was deposed, and a number of subsidiary dynasties were established in the Comoro Islands and elsewhere along the coast, each of which quickly established its existence independent of Kilwa, thus continuing the earlier patterns of Shirazi movements down the coast. And the peoples of the mainland remained an important factor in Kilwa politics. Husain b. Sulaiman (7) died fighting them.

The political development of Kilwa through the Shirazi and Mahdali dynasties was thus part of a process of increasing centralization, starting with a century of slow consolidation by a single *waungwana* family, followed by almost a century of increasing royal monopolization of wealth and institutionalization of royal authority. That this monopoly was not complete was revealed by the establishment of a new dynasty that was able to rule for the next 280 years but continued to be troubled by internal factionalization and threats from wealth and power held outside the ruling branch of the royal

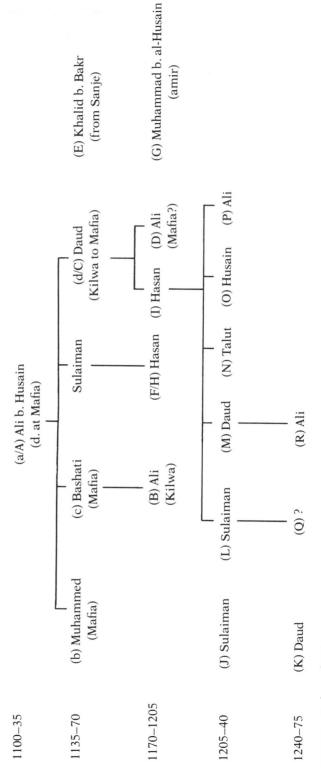

The Shirazi Dynasty

1100–35	(a/A) Ali b. Husain (d. at Mafia)	
1135–70	(b) Muhammed (Mafia)	Sulaiman	(d/C) Daud (Kilwa to Mafia)	(E) Khalid b. Bakr (from Sanje)
1170–1205	(c) Bashati (Mafia)	(F/H) Hasan	(I) Hasan	(D) Ali (Mafia?)	(G) Muhammad b. al-Husain (amir)
1205–40	(B) Ali (Kilwa)	(M) Daud	(N) Talut	(O) Husain	(P) Ali
1240–75	(L) Sulaiman	(Q) ?	(R) Ali		
	(J) Sulaiman	(K) Daud			

Fig. 11. Rulers of Kilwa

Fig. 11—*continued*

The Mahdali Dynasty

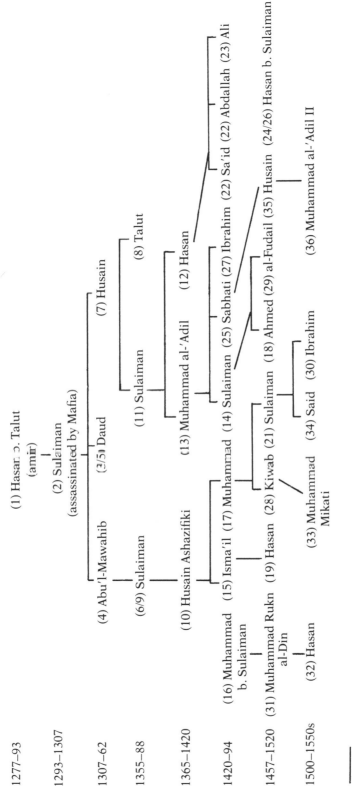

1277–93

1293–1307

1307–62

1355–88

1365–1420

1420–94

1457–1520

1500–1550s

Note: Lower-case letters = ruled on Mafia; capital letters = ruled on Kilwa. From Saad, "Kilwa Dynastic Historiography."

family as *waungwana* exerted influence and power within and without the government. The monarchy developed out of the oligarchic mode of government as wealth became concentrated in the hands of a single family, giving them great power that they were eventually able to convert into institutionalized authority, which of course they used to consolidate their position further through royal monopolies of trade and customs duties. That such families claimed foreign origins—whether as royals or as *sharifs*—was simply a further extension of *waungwana* hegemonic ideology to affirm the greater *baraka*, "blessing," and legitimacy of the ruling dynasty.

Politics of Symbols and Beliefs

Claims to prestigious origins were not the only means used to legitimate authority. Political authority has two main aspects: how power is wielded in exercise and maintenance of authority, and how the exercise of authority is made legitimate through shared symbols and symbolic actions, or rituals. If we wish to trace the centralization of power and the intitutionalization of authority, we must look at how it was done both in terms of the exercise of power and in terms of the ways the use of that power was projected as legitimate. We have already traced the ways in which the *waungwana* generally were able to control access to power and the ways in which certain *waungwana* families were then able to centralize that power into constituted authority. What remains is to see how symbols, rituals, and ideology were subtly transformed to reinforce the new order.

One element was the shift in the ideology of descent from the predominantly matrilineal mode revealed in the earliest periods in the traditions to the patrilineal mode revealed in the subsequent genealogies of kings. Matrilineal links continued to be important in many Swahili societies among farmers and land users, but prestigious *waungwana* families and royal families also traced their descent patrilineally. Thus a bilateral or cognatic kinship developed that was able to reckon inheritance and descent in different ways, the relative strength of the patrilineal mode increasing with the status of the individual. It was the development of this cognatic system that enabled the earliest Swahili migrants to establish local lineage connections rapidly through marriages to local women. It was this same system that enabled them to retain status later by restricting it to their own patrilineal descendants.

Certain general symbols of status were also converted to

restricted symbols of royalty. The ruler of Muqdisho in the four-teenth century wore a fashionable cloak, silk girdle, and turban and was accompanied by a silk canopy, drums, trumpets, and oboes. When Vasco da Gama later met the sultan of Malindi, the king wore a damask robe "trimmed with green satin and a rich turban," sat on a bronze throne beneath a canopy, and was accompanied by flutes and large, elaborately carved ivory side-blown horns, known as *siwa*. Each town had its own distinctive *siwa*—some ivory, some brass, and some wood—always elaborately carved or decorated.[23] Each identified the people for whom it was played as important members of the town. In nonroyal Swahili societies, any *waungwana* might wear fashionable clothes and have the *siwa*, flutes, drums, and cymbals played at initiations, marriages, or funerals. With the advent of royal rule, however, the use of *siwas* and other symbols of status became restricted to royalty. When the Vumba conquered the Shirazi towns to the south in the seventeenth century, the latter were prohibited from wearing any of the symbols of status and from using the *siwa*. The association of *siwas* with royalty came to be a test of legitimacy; he who held the *siwa* controlled the town. The Pate chronicle explains a disputed succession in terms of the ruling king refusing the use of the *siwa* for a boy's circumcision, whereupon the boy's mother had a second made, allowing anyone to use it. When the official *siwa* was later lost at sea the replacement was adopted, and the boy subsequently succeeded to the throne as the now legiti-mate heir.[24] In Kilwa an unsuccessful claimant to the throne alleg-edly threw the *siwa* into the sea in order to destroy kingship itself.[25] Much more recently, a British district officer in Pate confiscated the *siwa* to try to put an end to a series of succession disputes.[26] Finally, the Vumba *siwa* was a gift from Pate, symbolizing their status as clients of the Pate kings.

Royal rule was also consolidated through the use of titles setting the king apart and bringing prestige to his name. *Waungwana* arro-gated such honorary titles as *msharifu* (literally, "a descendant of the prophet") and *sheik* (a term of respect for a wise and pious man) to their own use as general terms of rank and status. Many rulers adopted these into their own names as well, but most also adopted a specific title restricted to kingship itself. The Swahili word for king or ruler, *mfalme* (whose use was first noted in the tenth century by al-Masudi in the older form *mfalume*), was sometimes used in this way, as was the Arabic/Persian *sheik/shehe/sheha*. The Bantu term *mwinyi* or *mwinyi mkuu* was widely used in the southern dialect area, and the Arabic *sultani* later gained wide use as well. Other rulers adopted distinctive titles: *fumo* in Pate, *seyyid* in Zanzibar, and *diwani* in Vumba and along the Mrima coast. The evolution of *diwani* is particularly interesting. The term generally means a councilor and was applied to lineage and ward elders who sat on town councils. But as the Vumba consolidated their rule, they adopted it as their own specific title, *Diwani,* revealing as they did so the evolution of royal rule itself from earlier patterns of rule by councilors.

The most powerful element adopted and adapted by royalty, however, was belief and ritual, both African and Islamic. For most Swahili, the worlds of the natural and the supernatural, of the physical and the moral, were one. Moral acts could and did have physical consequences. Moral actions and correct ritual observances insured social harmony, good health, abundant rainfalls, and fine harvests. Immoral acts or rituals slighted brought drought, famine, sickness, and death. People thus possessed extraordinary powers over the universe, powers they exercised through the spirits of their ancestors (*koma*). It was the ancestors who established society and the rules for proper social discourse, and their spirits continued to be part of the present social world. Immoral or antisocial behavior could be punished by an offended ancestor spirit's possessing the person and communicating through him the reasons for its distress, forcing the person to mend his or her ways. Nature spirits (*mizimu*) and malevolent spirits (*pepo*) also had to be accommodated. Nature spirits oversaw the fertility of the land and success in fishing, and their custodians were the descendants of the first settlers, or "owners of the land." Malevolent spirits, by contrast, could not be controlled; they could only be fought with powerful medicine. Human beings also had power over other human beings and were able to harm them by witchcraft or sorcery or to protect them with charms and spells. Belief and ritual action were thus active and interactive as people were in constant contact with spiritual forces and powers that insured their well-being. They were also personal and immediate, tied to the descendants and villages of the ancestors, to the fields they farmed, and to the waters they fished. Each village was a microcosm, a miniuniverse, with its own specific spirits associated with it. To move to another village was to enter another world.[27]

Many townspeople, however, operated in a wider world than the microcosm of the village, living in towns with other peoples, sailing from town to town along the coast, and trading with people from across the Indian Ocean. These people lived in a macrocosmic world inhabited by peoples speaking different languages, having different ancestors, and working in different occupations. In this world the beliefs of the microcosm were too parochial; what was needed were beliefs that were universal. And so townspeople began to adopt Islam, and in so doing they adopted a set of beliefs and a framework for action that were held in common by others in the town, by people in other towns, and by people from the whole Indian Ocean world.

We do not know how many people on the coast converted to Islam prior to 1500 or how deeply they embraced the new faith. The earliest coral mosques in Barawa, Zanzibar, Shanga, Muqdisho, Mafia, and Kilwa date from the twelfth and thirteenth centuries, and such mosques were not built in Ungwana until the fourteenth century and in Manda until the sixteenth, but earlier timber or mud and wattle mosques may have existed at any of these places. The use of Muslim jurisprudence is mentioned for Muqdisho in the fourteenth century, but a distinction remained between religious law overseen by the *qadi* and secular law administered by the council of elders. Battuta also reported that people in Mombasa and Kilwa were Shafi'i Muslim and that the ruler of Kilwa, Abu'l-Mawahib, was noted for his Muslim learning, piety, and charity, but we are told little about popular beliefs, and Portuguese accounts a century and a half later barely mention Islam. It is thus very unclear what impact Islam had on Swahili societies during the first four centuries of its existence in East Africa. The evidence seems to indicate that its impact was limited to traders, both local and foreign, who employed Islamic law and ethics to facilitate trade among the different people involved, and to prominent families for whom the wider community of Islam provided access to foreign trade and traders together with an identity that transcended local parochial loyalties.[28]

Linguistically, Swahili maintains a distinction today between indigenous religious concepts and Muslim ones. The words *koma*, *mizimu*, and *pepo* for ancestral, natural, and malevolent spirits, for example, all derive from proto-Swahili and proto-Sabaki words, as do most words associated with village, farming, and fishing activities. Words denoting Muslim religious, legal, and commercial concepts and institutions, however, are largely of Arabic provenance. Urban spirits are thus termed *jinn*, from the Arabic, while rural ones are *mizimu*. But few people occupied either the microcosmic world of the village or the macrocosmic one of the towns exclusively. Most operated in both, retaining aspects of both sets of beliefs. In the fields nature spirits had to be appeased, and newcomers to town had to acknowledge the powers of the original settlers over the welfare of the land, while in the towns people attended local mosques dedicated to the well-being of the ward. The two sets of beliefs coexisted interdependently into the twentieth century, when Muslim clerics were still consulted for Quranic charms to ward off witchcraft.[29] Boys' initiations followed the traditional pattern of ritual seclusion overseen by traditional *makungwi* authorities but were preceded by circumcision by the Muslim *mwalimu* and ended with a Muslim *maulidi* reading and *sadaka* feast.[30] Prominent Muslims were still buried in elaborate stone tombs, at which their descendants burned incense and made sacrifices to appease the ancestors.[31]

Waungwana could accommodate diverse ritual responsibilities simply by allocating responsibilities to different lineages and wards in the community. But kings, especially merchant kings, had to bridge all worlds of belief if they were to fulfill their roles as guardians of whole communities. On the one hand, they personified the macrocosm, overseeing diverse ethnic communities and actively engaging in commerce, but on the other, they had to see to the needs of each individual ritual community. To fulfill the first, they appealed to their status as *sharifs*, or as pious men. The rulers of Pate, Vumba, and Kilwa all claimed *sharif* ancestry. To fulfill the second, they either acknowledged the ritual powers of subgroups within the society or partook of their rituals themselves. The Vumba *sharifs* performed rain magic for the neighboring Digo and Segeju while maintaining their standing as pious Muslims within Vumba itself.[32]

In transcending individual lineages and wards, the kings unified Swahili societies and provided links to the wider coastal world. In transcending parochial spirits, they unified beliefs. But, like all Swahili, they were able to accomplish this only by building on their own traditions while borrowing selectively from others to create a dynamic synthesis that was uniquely Swahili.

From Village to State: Seven Centuries of Swahili History

The Swahili were less a people than a historical phenomenon as peoples along the coast traded, interacted, migrated, settled, and developed more complex structures over a period of seven centuries to form the distinctive culture we know as Swahili today. The Shirazi were the prototypical Swahili, born among the peoples of the northern coast toward the end of the first millennium and raised along the fringes of the coast, where their development was affected by the sea and a slowly developing international trading economy. Swahili villages, like those of the Bajuni today, were homogeneous farming and fishing communities, but towns growing prosperous from trade attracted migrants from the mainland, from elsewhere along the coast, and from overseas to become more economically differentiated and heterogeneous urban communities. Living on the sea, the Swahili became a highly mobile people, easily and safely traversing great distances. Once the development of Swahili culture had begun in the north, it rapidly spread down the coast as people sought new opportunities in the trading entrepôts of the south. What distinguished the early Swahili from their neighbors was not alien origins or an alien culture but the phenomenon of a maritime trading diaspora and the urbanization, economic differentiation, and social stratification that resulted from trade and migration.

Village societies had been unified, with people in the villages sharing common languages, occupations, styles of living, ancestors, beliefs, and values. All were related by bonds of kinship, enabling village elders to meet informally to adjudicate disputes. In towns, however, people came from different ethnic groups speaking different languages and having a diverse range of occupations, styles of living, beliefs, and values. Villages became wards within larger towns; lineage politics became the art of constructing complex personal networks of cognates, allies, and clients; egalitarian values gave way to values of status and rank; and leadership became the politics of competing factions and traditions as older inhabitants sought to consolidate their power against newer arrivals. Competition between different lineages, wards, peoples, values, and traditions within a common framework of Swahili language, history, and culture constituted a social order that bound townspeople together in interdependent wholes.

As trade expanded and grew in the first half of the second millennium, greater wealth became concentrated in the hands of a few families, who were then able to increase their power and to consolidate it in institutions of royal authority. Wealth provided the means, but family traditions, ritual power, and superior piety gave legitimacy to the new institutions. The politics of faction became the politics of class and of religion as ruling classes adopted the universal values of Islam to transcend and embrace the parochialities of local situations. Social stratification gave way to polar divisions between rulers and ruled. But the centralization of authority was never able to supplant totally the powers of the different constituent parts; "owners of the land" continued to exercise spiritual power, and councils of elders moderated the powers of kings.

Politically, the coast remained fragmented. Even at the height of Kilwa's power, for example, it exerted only nominal suzerainty over related dynasties in other towns in the region. What gave coherence to Swahili society, enabling us to use the term for such widely scattered and diverse communities, were the common historical experiences, reflected in their traditions, that produced their language and culture. It is a complex history, consisting of many strands. We have been able to unravel only a few but enough, we trust, to give some idea of what the whole fabric in all its complexity and diversity must have looked like.

APPENDIX I

Major Sound Changes Differentiating Swahili/Elwana from Comorian/Mijikenda/Pokomo

Swahili/Elwana	Comorian/Mijikenda/Pokomo	Proto-Bantu
p	(p >) bilabial > h	*p
t (Elwana dental t̲)	(t >) r > rolled alveolar fricative > h	*t
ch (> dental t̲)	ts	*c
nj (> dental nd̲)	ndz	*nj

Examples

Stand. Swahili: *-paka* 'smear,' *-poa* 'cool,' *-punguza* 'diminish'
Comorian (Ngazija): *-βaha, -βoa, -βunguza*
Mijikenda (Giryama): *-haka, -hola, -hunguza*
Stand. Swahili: *-tambaa* 'crawl,' *-tetema* 'shiver,' *-tota* 'sink'
Comorian: *-ramba(y)a, -rerema, -rora*
Mijikenda (Giryama): *-hambala, -hehema, -hoha*
Stand. Swahili: *nchi* 'country,' *-choma* 'burn,' *chui* 'leopard'
Northern Swahili: *nt'i, -toma, t'ui*
Mijikenda (Giryama): *tsi, -tsoma, tsui*
Stand. Swahili: *njaa* 'hunger,' *nje* 'outside,' *njoo* 'come'
Northern Swahili: *nd̲aa, nd̲e, nd̲oo*
Mijikenda (Giryama): *ndzala, ndze, ndzoo*

---

*See D. Nurse, "Is Comorian Swahili?" Round Table on the Limits of Swahili, Paris, 1983.

APPENDIX 2

Major Sound Changes Differentiating Northern and Southern Swahili Dialects

All northern dialects show early innovation of (dental) nd from nj, and (dental) t from ch.

Examples

Southern Dialect (Unguja)	Northern Dialect (Amu)
-vunja 'break'	*-vunda*
nje 'outside'	*nde*
njia 'path'	*ndia*
mchanga 'sand'	*mtanga*
nchi 'country'	*nt'i*
-chukua 'carry'	*-tukua*

Northern dialects also lose /g/. Because the Mombasa sub-dialects and Chifunzi are near the border between northern and southern dialects, they have borrowed much vocabulary over the centuries, resulting in a mixed situation, so it is not clear if they share this loss or not.

Southern Dialect	Northern Dialect
-gawanya 'distribute'	*-awanya*
figo 'kidney'	*nso*
-gumu 'hard'	*-umu*

There are also consistent differences in the verb systems of the northern and southern Swahili dialects. For details of these, see Nurse, "A Tentative Classification of the Primary Dialects of Swahili," *SUGIA* 4 (1982):165–205.

APPENDIX 3

Major Sound Changes Differentiating the Northern Swahili Dialects Internally

3a. Differentiating Mombasa and Chifunzi from the Remaining Northern Dialects

The northern dialects of northern Kenya and Somalia develop /s/, /z/ where Mombasa, Chifunzi, and most other Sabaki languages have /f/, /v/ respectively. They also weaken /j/ to /y/ or zero.

Examples

Mombasa, Chifunzi, Southern Dialects	Remaining Northern Dialects
-fika 'arrive'	-sikilia
figo 'kidney'	nso, iso
-finyanga 'mold pottery'	-sinyanga
wavuvi 'fishermen'	wavuzi
vyote, vyosi 'all'	zot'e
vit'u 'things'	zit'u
-ja 'come'	-va
jongoo 'millipede'	yongoo
juzi 'two days ago'	yuzi
-je 'how?'	-(y)e
jino 'tooth'	(y)ino

The first two changes are also shared by all Comorian dialects.

3b. Differentiating Miini from the Remaining Northern Dialects

Miini retains /nz/ and /ł/, and the remaining northern dialects develop /nd/ and lose /ł/.

Miini	Remaining Northern Dialects
-aanza 'begin'	-anda
mapenzi 'love'	mapendi

kanzi 'treasure'	*kandi*
-łangala 'look at'	*-angalia*
łeeło 'today'	*(y)eo*
-łuma 'bite'	*-uma*
mbeełe 'in front'	*mbee*

There are also certain differences between the verb system of Miini and that of the remaining northern dialects. See chap. 3, n. 7, and D. Nurse, "The Swahili Dialects of Somalia and the Northern Kenya Coast," in M.-F. Rombi, ed., *Etudes sur le Bantu oriental* (Paris, 1982), pp. 73–121.

3c. Differentiating Bajuni from the Remaining Northern Dialects

Bajuni differs from the remaining northern dialects by dropping nasals (= m, n, etc.) before some consonants and having /s/ where remaining dialects have /sh/.

Bajuni	Remaining Northern Dialects
isi 'fish'	*nsi*
it'i 'country'	*nt'i*
vua 'rain'	*mvua*
jisi 'kind'	*jinsi*
mosi 'smoke'	*moshi*
singo 'neck'	*shingo*
-kumbusa 'remind'	*-kumbusha*

Bajuni also developed /dh/ and /ch/ from earlier /z/ and /t/, respectively, and these features have transferred themselves also to Siu and Pate.

Bajuni (Siu, Pate)	Amu
mbudhi 'goat'	*mbuzi*
mwedhi 'moon'	*mwezi*
ndhi 'root'	*mzi*
dhich'u 'things'	*zit'u*
-chachu 'three'	*-tatu*
ncho 'river'	*mto*
ichunda 'fruit'	*tunda*

APPENDIX 4

Major Sound Changes Differentiating Southern Swahili Dialects Internally

4a. Differentiating Mwani from Other Southern Dialects

Apart from archaisms (such as the retention of /l/), doubtless retained because of its isolated position, Mwani differs from other southern dialects by changes mainly induced by contact with Makonde and/or Makua. Mwani has /s/ where the other southern dialects have /ch/; Mwani has lost /g/; from older sequences of nasal (= m, n, etc.) followed by certain consonants, Mwani keeps the nasal, whereas the other southern dialects keep the consonant. As far as can be judged from the limited data available, Mgao behaves like Mwani in these cases.

Examples

Southern Dialects	Mwani	Mgao	
mchanga 'sand'	*nsanga*	*nsanga*	
-cheza 'play'	*-seza*		
jicho 'eye'	*riso*		
kichwa 'head'	*kiswa*		
mboga 'vegetable'	*mboa*		
mgongo 'back'	*myongo*	*mongo*	
mbegu 'seed'	*mbeu*	*mbeu*	
pete 'ring'	*mete*		older **mpete*
pua 'nose'	*mula*	*mula*	other **mpula*
mtu 'person'	*munu*	*munu*	older **muntu*
tatu 'three' (class 10)	*natu*		older **ntatu*

4b. Differentiating Vumba and Makunduchi from Remaining Southern Dialects

Where all other Swahili dialects have /p/, Vumba and some sub-dialects of Makunduchi (also Chifunzi) have developed bilabial /β/. The northern subdialects of Makunduchi (e.g., Paje) have /p/, whereas the southern ones (e.g., Jambiani) have /β/. This bilabial also appears in Comorian.

Vumba	Other Southern Dialects	Comorian
-βaka 'smear'	-paka	-βaha
-βeleka 'send'	-peleka	-βeleha
-βika 'cook'	-pika	-βiha
-βoa 'cool down'	-poa	-βoa
-βuzia 'blow'	-puliza	-βuza

4c. Differentiating Vumba from Makunduchi

Where most other Swahili dialects have /t/, Vumba (and Chifunzi) has developed /r/. This /r/ also appears in Comorian.

Vumba	Makunduchi	Comorian
-raβika 'vomit'	-taβika	-raβiha
-rerema 'shiver'	-tetema	-rerema
mri 'tree'	mti	mri
moro 'fire'	moto	moro
-ruma 'send'	-tuma	-ruma

See D. Nurse, "A Historical View of the Southern Dialects of Swahili," *SUGIA* 6 (1984).

APPENDIX 5

Features Shared by Swahili and Comorian in General, and the Northern Swahili Dialects and Comorian in Particular

5*a*. Swahili and Comorian

The features shared by Swahili and Comorian are few and point to a short period of interaction. Where Mijikenda and Lower Pokomo have /dz/, Swahili and Comorian show a weakening, whose stages are /j/ (southern Swahili, Ngazija, Mwali) > /ʒ/ (older Bajuni, Ndzwani, Maore) > /y/ (northern Swahili minus Mombasa and Chifunzi) > zero (northern Swahili, before front vowels). See Appendix 3*a*.

Examples

Southern Swahili (Unguja): *-ja* 'come,' *-je* 'how,' *-jua* 'know'
Ndzwani: *-ʒa, -ʒe, -ʒua*
Northern Swahili: *-ya, -(y)e, -yua*

As pointed out in chapter 1, all Swahili dialects, except Mwani, and some Comorian indicate "future" by cognate forms in -ta-, -ṯa-, -cha-, -tso-.

5*b*. Northern Swahili and Comorian

Where all other Sabaki languages have /f/, /v/, northern Swahili, (minus Mombasa and Chifunzi) and Comorian have /s/, /z/, respectively. See Appendix 3*a*.

Comorian and northern Swahili lose inherited /g/. See Appendix 2.

There are also certain parallel innovations between parts of the northern Swahili and Comorian verb systems. However, since those which appear in all the northern dialects do not occur in all Comorian dialects, or vice versa, they are best considered as later loans.

APPENDIX 6

Features Shared by Comorian and the Southern Swahili Dialects and Assumed to Result from a Period of Early Contact on the Tanzanian Coast

Features shared by Comorian and Vumba and Chifunzi (and Ma-kunduchi) are discussed in Appendix 4*b*, 4*c*.

Common to the verb systems of Comorian and all the southern dialects except Mwani are three striking innovations, which occur nowhere else in Sabaki or eastern Bantu:

1. A past or perfect tense marked by a vowel harmony suffix

Southern Dialect (Matele, Pemba)	Comorian	(Stand. Swahili)
tu-aw-a 'we went out'	*ri-law-a*	*tuliondoka*
tu-end-e 'we went'	*ri-end-e*	*tulikwenda*
tu-pit-i 'we passed'	*ri-βir-i*	*tulipita*
tu-on-o 'we saw'	*ri-on-o*	*tuliona*
tu-fung-u 'we closed'	*ri-fung-u*	*tulifunga*

2. A present negative marked by the same suffix but different prefixes

Southern Dialect	Comorian	(Stand. Swahili)
k'atu-aw-a 'we don't go out'	*kari-law-a*	hatuondoki
k'atu-end-e 'we don't go'	*kari-end-e*	hatuendi
k'atu-pit-i 'we don't pass'	*kari-βir-i*	hatupiti
k'atu-on-o 'we don't see'	*kari-on-o*	hatuoni
k'atu-fung-u 'we don't close'	*kari-fung-u*	hatufungi

3. The fact that both the above always cooccur in all the dialects in which they are present

APPENDIX 7

Proto-Swahili Vocabulary

On the basis of cognate words in northern and southern Swahili dialects, we may reconstruct the following items for proto-Swahili. The objects or activities to which these items refer were therefore known to, or used by, the proto-Swahili. Actual proto-Swahili forms are not quoted. Northern dialect items are usually cited in the Amu dialect, southern dialect items in Unguja. A question mark (?) means that there is some doubt about whether the line can be assigned to proto-Swahili or the other named source, and parentheses mean a borrowed, i.e., noncognate, item. The order of presentation roughly follows that of chapter 4.

Northern Dialects	Southern Dialects
mtumbwi 'dugout canoe'	*mtumbwi* ?
mtepe 'sewn boat'	*mtepe* ?
k'asi, k'asis 'oar, paddle'	*k'afi*
nsi 'fish'	*swi*
ng'amba 'hawkshead turtle'	*ng'amba* ?
k'usu 'sp. turtle'	*k'usu* ?
mngumi 'whale'	*mngumi, mnyagumi* ?
kioo 'fishhook'	*ndoana, kiroo*
mshipi 'fishing line'	*mshipi*
-va, -ova 'to fish using line'	*-loa*
(other Sabaki *-vua*) 'to fish'	*-vua*
ukondo 'fish spear'	*konjo, konzo* 'spear'
(other Sabaki *mgono*) 'fish-trap'	*mgono*
ema 'fish basket'	*lema, dema* < Persian ?
wavu 'fishing net'	*wavu* < Persian ?
mtama 'sorghum'	*mtama* < Southern Cushitic
mawee 'bulrush millet'	*mawele* < Central Sudanic ?
wimbi 'finger millet'	(*wimbi*)
	gimbi 'millet beer'
mpunga 'rice'	*mpunga*
mtee 'rice grain'	*mchele*

wali 'cooked rice'   (wali)
                                        ugali 'mush'
mbaazi 'pigeon pea'   mbaazi, mbalazi ?
Bajuni t'ooko, Miini ntoloko   cho(r)oko 'green gram'
'cowpea'
k'unde 'sp. bean'   k'unde
yungu 'pumpkin'   Mwani ungu
tanga 'cucumber'   tango
tikiti 'watermelon'   tikiti ?
t'enga 'small grain of rice,'   chenga
etc.
Bajuni kisike 'ear, cob of   suke ?
corn,' etc.
t'upa now 'bottle,' formerly   ch'upa
'gourd'
muwa, unyuwa 'sugarcane'   muwa
ufuta 'simsim'   ufuta
mwono 'castor oil plant'   mbono
izu 'banana'   (other Sabaki izu) Southern
                                        Cushitic 'ensete'

nazi 'coconut'   nazi ?
mkindu 'wild date palm'   mkindu
unga 'flour'   unga
mtuzi 'relish'   mchuzi
mataza 'soup, curry,   machaza ?
porridge'
(mboga) 'vegetable'   mboga
munyu 'salt'   munyu
t'embo 'palm wine'   t'embo ?
upanga 'machete'   upanga
kitoka 'ax'   shoka
kisu 'knife'   kifyu
t'ezo 'adze'   t'ezo ?
yembe 'hoe'   jembe
kinu 'mortar'   kinu
mt'i 'pestle'   mchi
-lima 'cultivate'   -lima
-timba 'dig'   -chimba
-palia 'weed, scrape'   -palia
mbeu 'seed'   mbegu
-vuna 'harvest'   -vuna
utaa 'grain store'   uchaga ?

-*pepet'a* 'winnow'	-*pepet'a*
uteo 'winnowing tray'	(other Sabaki *lutseo,* etc.)
-*twa* 'grind'	-*twanga* 'pound'
-*ponda* 'pound'	-*ponda*
-*paaza* 'grind'	-*paaza*
k'onde 'cultivated field'	*k'onde* ?
munda 'cultivated field'	*mgunda*
Bajuni -*pua* 'thresh'	-*pura*
	upuzi 'chaff'
wishwa, wisha 'chaff'	*wishwa* ?
k'uku 'chicken'	*k'uku*
k'oo 'hen, breeding bird'	*k'oo* < Central Sudanic ?
ngamia, Miini *ngamiiła*	*ngamia* < Arabic
'camel'	
ng'ombe 'cow'	*ng'ombe*
mbuzi 'goat'	*mbuzi*
(i)*mbwa* 'dog'	*mbwa*
p'aka 'cat'	*p'aka*
-*kama* 'milk'	-*kama*
-*umika* 'bleed by cupping'	-*umika*
ziwa 'milk'	*maziwa* < Southern Cushitic
-*sukasuka* 'churn'	-*sukasuka* < Southern Cushitic
kiwee 'udder'	*kiwele*
zizi 'cattle pen'	*zizi* ?
-*lisa, -lisha* 'graze'	-*lisha*
-*tasa* 'barren'	-*tasa* < Southern Cushitic
uta 'bow'	*uta*
muvi 'arrow'	*mvi*
wano '(arrow) shaft'	*wano*
upote 'bowstring'	*upote* ?
chembe 'arrowhead'	*chembe* ?
utungu 'poison'	*uchungu*
fumo 'spear'	*fumo*
ngao 'shield'	*shield*
uti 'shaft'	*uti*
-*winda* 'hunt'	-*winja*

For "trap" and "sling," the northern and southern forms are not cognate; nevertheless, both can be assumed for proto-Swahili as the northern and the southern forms have cognates elsewhere in Sabaki.

-fua 'forge'	*-fua*
mfuzi 'smith,' etc.	*mfua*
chuma 'iron'	*chuma*
nyundo, nundo 'hammer'	*nyundo*
mvuo 'bellows'	*mvuo*
-vukuta 'blow bellows'	*-vukuta*
fuawe 'anvil'	*fuawe*
k'weleo 'tongs'	*k'oleo* ?
-sinyanga 'make pottery'	*-finyanga*
msinyandi 'potter'	*mfinyanzi*
uwongo etc. 'clay for pots'	*udongo*
ny-ungu etc. 'cooking pot'	*ny-ungu, ch-ungu, j-ungu,* etc.
mtungi 'water pot'	*mtungi* < Persian
ubia 'pot'	*(ki)bia, (ki)biga*
kijaya 'potsherd'	*kigaa, kigae*

See D. Nurse, "A Hypothesis Concerning the Origin of Swahili," *Azania* 18 (1983).

ABBREVIATIONS

AARP	*Art and Archaeology Research Papers*
IJAHS	*International Journal of African Historical Studies*
JAH	*Journal of African History*
JRAI	*Journal of the Royal Anthropological Institute*
SUGIA	*Sprache und Geschichte in Afrika*
TNR	*Tanganyika/Tanzania Notes and Records*

NOTES

Chapter 1: Swahili and Their History

1. J. Strandes, *The Portuguese Period in East Africa* (Nairobi, 1961), p. 74.

2. P. S. Garlake, *The Early Islamic Architecture of the East African Coast* (Nairobi, 1966), p. 2.

3. N. Chittick, "The Coast before the Arrival of the Portuguese," in B. A. Ogot, ed., *Zamani* (Nairobi, 1973), pp. 112–13.

4. *Sunday Nation* (Nairobi), 11 December 1977.

5. M. Metzler, "The Near East and East Africa: An Initial Investigation into Settlement Patterns through Ceramic Dating," University of Nairobi, Department of History seminar paper, 1978.

6. N. Chittick, *Kilwa: An Islamic Trading City on the East African Coast* (Nairobi, 1974).

7. M. Horton, *Shanga 1980* (Cambridge, 1980).

8. D. W. Phillipson, "Some Iron Age Sites in the Lower Tana Valley," *Azania* 14 (1979): 155–62; M. Horton, personal communication.

9. al-Idrisi, in G. S. P. Freeman-Grenville, *The East African Coast: Select Documents from the First Century to the Early Nineteenth Century* (Oxford, 1962), p. 20.

10. T. H. Wilson, "Settlement Patterns on the Coast of Southern Somalia and Kenya," First International Congress of Somali Studies, Muqdisho, 1980.

11. The following is compiled from J. M. Bujra, "An Anthropological Study of Political Action in a Bajuni Village in Kenya" (Ph.D. thesis, London, 1968); A. P. Caplan, *Choice and Constraint in a Swahili Community* (London, 1975); R. L. Pouwels, "Islam and Islamic Leadership in the Coastal Communities of Eastern Africa, 1700–1914" (Ph.D. thesis, Los Angeles, 1979); A. H. J. Prins, *The Swahili-speaking Peoples of Zanzibar and the East African Coast* (London, 1967); idem, *Didemic Lamu* (Groningen, 1971); A. el Zein, *The Sacred Meadows* (Evanston, Ill., 1974); G. M. Shepherd, "Two Marriage Forms in the Comoro Islands: An Investigation," *Africa* 47 (1977): 344–59; and P. Lienhardt, *The Medicine Man* (Oxford, 1968).

12. Most of the early documents referring to the coast are published in Freeman-Grenville, *East African Coast*, though the collection and translations vary greatly in quality.

13. al-Masudi and ibn Battuta, in ibid., pp. 14–16, 27–31.

14. The problems of interpreting oral traditions are discussed in J. C. Miller, ed., *The African Past Speaks* (Folkestone, 1980), and summarized in T. Spear, "Oral Traditions: Whose History?" *History in Africa* 8 (1981): 163–79.

Chapter 2: The African Background of Swahili

1. We use the term "Swahili" as a descriptive term for the members of historical Swahili-speaking communities. Swahili normally identify themselves by the name of their town, by their lineage or quarter within the town, or by general cultural terms such as "Shirazi." For the debate on identifying the Swahili, see C. M. Eastman, "Who Are the Waswahili?" *Africa* 41 (1971): 228–36; I. N. Shariff, "Waswahili and Their Language: Some Misconceptions," *Kiswahili* 43 (1973): 67–75; and M. Tolmacheva, "The Origin of the Name 'Swahili,'" *TNR* 77/78 (1976): 27–37.

2. C. Ehret, *Ethiopians and East Africans* (Nairobi, 1974); idem, *The Historical Reconstruction of Southern Cushitic Phonology and Vocabulary* (Berlin, 1980); C. Ehret and M. Posnansky, eds., *The Archaeological and Linguistic Reconstruction of African History* (San Francisco, 1982).

3. In this account we have ignored the Nilotic languages spoken by peoples as diverse as the Luo (Western Nilotes: Uganda, western Kenya, and Tanzania), the Maasai (Eastern Nilotes: central Kenya and Tanzania), and the Dadog and Kalenjin (Southern Nilotes: western Tanzania and Kenya). Emerging from the southern Sudan, the earliest of these immigrants, the Southern Nilotes, had reached northern Kenya by the close of the last millennium B.C. and then turned south into Kenya and Tanzania. They were soon followed by Eastern Nilotes and, at the beginning of the present millennium, by Western Nilotes. The Southern Nilotes were not very different culturally from the Southern Cushites who had preceded them south. Nilotic migrations and subsequent settlements are not dealt with here because they had little formative effect on the peoples of the coastal region. They settled mainly in central and western East Africa, and only limited Nilotic influence ever filtered down to the coast through intervening communities.

4. Within any area where related languages are spoken, if we find one part, often small, where there is a high level of linguistic differentiation and another part, often much larger, where there is more homogeneity, we assume that the former is likely to be the earlier homeland whence communities dispersed through the latter. The British Isles, whence English spread, contain a high concentration of different dialects in a small space, whereas the countries to which English expanded in the course of a few centuries—North America, Australia, South Africa—are much bigger geographically but relatively less differentiated linguistically. The Bantu languages of most of equatorial and southern Africa are relatively similar to each other. On the other hand, the Bantu languages in the northwestern part of the territory, in eastern Nigeria, Cameroon, Gabon, Congo, and parts of Zaire, are much less similar, both to each other and to Bantu languages elsewhere. Furthermore, the languages to which the Bantu group is most closely connected are spoken in adjacent parts of Cameroon and southeastern Nigeria. Thus the Bantu homeland was most probably located in that area.

5. The word for "cow" (-*gombe*) is almost universal in eastern and

southern Bantu languages today but occurs in irregular form in the northwest, indicating that cattle keeping may derive from early contact with central Sudanic peoples north of the equatorial forest. Central Sudanic languages are distantly related to Nilotic and are today spoken in parts of Uganda and Zaire to the west.

6. T. Spear, *Kenya's Past* (London, 1981), pp. 29–33.

7. The evidence for this is only suggestive, however, since three of the four Bantu groups now residing in the northeast—Rufiji-Ruvuma, Chaga-Taita, and Thagicu—are linguistic isolates not easily related to other groups of Bantu languages in eastern Africa. Only the fourth group, Northeast Coast Bantu, is clearly related to other Bantu groups to the southwest.

8. D. Nurse and C. Ehret, "The Taita Cushites," *SUGIA* 3 (1981): 125–68.

9. This gap may not be serious since there are sites on the edges of the hills with ceramics dating from the first millennium. John Sutton, personal communication.

10. D. Nurse, "Bantu Migration into East Africa: Linguistic Evidence," and R. C. Soper, "Bantu Migration into East Africa: Archaeological Evidence," both in Ehret and Posnansky, *Archaeological and Linguistic Reconstruction.*

11. In fact, the southern Swahili do have such traditions, but they are heavily disguised by Shirazi mythology. See chapter 4.

12. D. Nurse, "On Dating Swahili," *Etudes Ocean Indien* 2 (1983): 59–72.

Chapter 3: The Emergence of the Swahili-Speaking Peoples

1. It is important to realize that neat tree diagrams such as that used in figure 7 are not intended to be a representation of cultural evolution or of later linguistic development. They are a classificatory device and represent only a linguistic hypothesis about the development of dialects based on certain examples of sound changes. They tend to emphasize the importance of protolanguages and protoperiods and to deemphasize subsequent developments. As we shall see, the northern and southern dialects of Swahili have been separate for more than a thousand years, whereas the proto-Sabaki and proto-Swahili periods together probably lasted less than five hundred. Since all the Sabaki languages have been evolving for more than a thousand years, why, by any criteria, have northern and southern Swahili remained more similar to each other than to any of the other Sabaki languages? The answer lies in the events of the last millennium. Once the initial association of Swahili-speaking communities with the coast had occurred in late proto-Sabaki times, the phenomena and influences to which they were all exposed, particularly between 800 and 1500, served as a cohesive rather than as a divisive force. The effect of trading along the entire coast, the prosperity that this engendered, outside cultural influences, the interrelatedness of

many coastal families, and the universality of Islam all served to bind the coastal communities together. Until very recently, Swahili traders, sailors, fishermen, and clergy traveled the length of the coast, from Muqdisho to Lamu to Mombasa to Zanzibar to Kilwa to Madagascar and the Comoro Islands.

2. The Pokomo referred to here is essentially Lower Pokomo. Upper Pokomo reveals a mixed situation, crisscrossed by isoglosses, with the northern and southern parts resembling Elwana and Lower Pokomo, respectively.

3. Such as Marika (spelled variously Marica, Marique, Merca) and Makaya (Macaia).

4. T. Spear, *The Kaya Complex: A History of the Mijikenda Peoples of the Kenya Coast to 1900* (Nairobi, 1978), pp. 16–43.

5. Horton, *Shanga 1980;* Phillipson, "Some Iron Age Sites."

6. H. Sassoon, "Excavations at the Site of Early Mombasa," *Azania* 15 (1980): 1–44; Wilson, "Settlement Patterns."

7. In the verb systems of Miini, Pokomo, and Mijikenda there are two striking innovations that seem to indicate contact between them at an early point. One is the negative marker /nta-/. All Sabaki mark negative by a prefix derivable from *nka-: Stand. Swahili /ha-/, Mwani /a-/, Comorian /ka-/, Pemba /k'a-/, etc. (see Appendixes 2 and 6). But Pokomo, Elwana, Miini, and Digo have a second marker in /nta-/, which is an innovation and not derivable from /nka-/, e.g., Miini *nta-chinakhteka* 'we are not laughing,' *nta-shkuteka* 'we didn't laugh.' In Pokomo and Digo it occurs in predictable complementary distribution with /nka-/, whereas in Miini it appears to occur haphazardly. The fact that it occurs in all Pokomo in a predictable pattern, but only in Miini of the Swahili dialects and in Digo of the Mijikenda dialects, points to an origin in Pokomo.

The second is the "present" marker /-na-/. All Sabaki used to indicate "present" by a marker /-a-/. All the Mijikenda, Lower Pokomo, Miini, and southern dialects of Zanzibar Island have innovated -/na-/. The fact that it occurs in all the Mijikenda, but only in Lower Pokomo and Miini of the northern Swahili dialects, points to an origin in Mijikenda. Both of these are innovations; both occur in Miini; but neither seems to originate in Miini. The conclusion is that they were transferred to Miini from Mijikenda or (Lower) Pokomo at a time when they were in contact, that is, when Miini was used as a lingua franca between Miini-speaking townspeople and Mijikenda-Pokomo-speaking farmers in the hinterland of Barawa. See D. Nurse, "Linguistic Evidence for Shungwaya," First International Congress of Somali Studies, Muqdisho, 1980.

8. The evidence that Bajuni has been influenced by Dahalo and Somali-Aweera comes partly from the sound system but mainly from vocabulary. Bajuni replaces inherited /z/ by /dh/, and some speakers replace /s/ by /th/. Dahalo and Somali-Aweera have no /z/ or /s/ but have /dh/ and /th/ (or dental equivalents) instead. Bajuni, and to a much lesser extent the other northern dialects, has a large number of words visibly taken from a Somali or Aweera dialect: *abawa* 'older brother,' *abaya* 'older sister,' *avu* 'maternal

uncle,' *avuru* 'strong man,' *barobaro* 'young man,' *bishee* 'sp. millet,' *bodo* 'porridge,' *buru* 'maize,' *damari* 'beestings,' *-dara* 'touch,' *doko* 'anus,' *duko* 'deaf,' *dhela* 'bucket,' *-fura* 'swell,' *-gura* 'move above,' *havule* 'unmarried girl,' *mshobo* 'dandy,' etc.

9. There is also a pocket of aging Swahili-speakers on the northwest coast of Madagascar near Nosse Be. Their Swahili is so like Unguja that it would seem to be a result of a recent migration from Zanzibar. There are also reports of a second pocket farther south down the west coast of Madagascar, but nothing more is known of them.

10. The reasons for this lie neither in the vocabulary nor in the sound system of Mwani but in its verb system. Its vocabulary shows a low statistical relationship with other southern dialects, partly the result of retaining older items but mainly the result of absorbed material from Makonde and/or Makua. There is no real way as yet of dating this material. Similarly, the ways in which its (and Mgao's) inherited sound system differs from the other southern dialects are the result of archaisms and Makonde influence. Again, there is no sound way of dating these, other than noting that some (e.g., the processes that have affected sequences of nasal plus voiceless consonant) imply considerable age.

The verb systems of all the other southern dialects show differences from the northern dialects. Most of these are innovations; one or two are retentions of older features. Mwani shows none of the innovations but does retain the inherited features. In other words, the innovations developed after Mwani split off. Further, the southern dialects share certain innovations with Comorian (see Appendix 6), which are presumably the result of interaction at an early point on the Tanzania coast. Since Mwani does not share these, it must have split before the Comorians reached the southern coast.

Since what is known about Mwani, Mgao, or the Mozambique coast is insufficient, we do not deal with them further here. It should be noted, however, that the Chibwene archaeological site farther south is dated to the ninth century.

11. Linguistically, the earliest settlement in the south might have been in either the Vumba-Mtang'ata or the Zanzibar-Pemba dialect area. Our choice of Kilwa is based on the antiquity of the site and its traditions of settlement from the north, as detailed below.

12. Mtang'ata here, as in the previous figure, includes Mtang'ata and "Lugha ya Zamani."

13. Chittick, *Kilwa.*

14. G. M. Shepherd, "The Making of the Swahili: A View from the Southern End of the East African Coast," *Paideuma* 28 (1982): 129–48.

15. ibn Battuta, in Freeman-Grenville, *East African Coast*, p. 31.

16. al-Idrisi, in ibid., pp. 19–20.

17. D. Nurse, "A Tentative Classification of the Primary Dialects of Swahili," *SUGIA* 4 (1982): 165–205.

18. Said Bakari bin Sultani Ahmed, *The Swahili Chronicle of Ngazija*, trans. and ed. L. Harries (Bloomington, Ind., 1977).

Chapter 4: Early Swahili Society, 800–1100

1. The following was compiled from: Wilson, "Settlement Patterns"; Horton, *Shanga 1980;* N. Chittick, "Report on Excavations at Manda, 1978," *Nyame Akuma* 14 (1979): 20–22; idem, *Kilwa;* al-Masudi and al-Idrisi, in Freeman-Grenville, *East African Coast,* pp. 14–17, 19–20; and from proto-Swahili vocabulary reconstructed in Appendix 7.

2. al-Masudi, in Freeman-Grenville, *East African Coast,* pp. 14, 16.

3. The traditions analyzed here and in chapter 5 are ones that have been collected by a number of people from the Portuguese period on and include both traditions collected orally and translations of Swahili manuscripts (themselves redactions of earlier oral accounts). They are very uneven in quality and do not adhere to modern scholarly standards regarding the systematic collection of traditions; thus they are difficult to interpret in any uniform way. The earliest collections date from the early sixteenth century, but most derive from the late nineteenth and early twentieth centuries. All concern events that occurred from five to nine centuries before. None can thus be expected to convey accurately the specific events of the time. Rather, they represent the attempt by Swahili to derive meaning from their historical past to explain how modern society developed. This does not present the historical problem it may seem to, since our chronological and detailed data come from archaeological, documentary, and linguistic sources, and we are using the traditions to explore the evolution of Swahili institutions, as discussed in chapter 1. Many of the traditions are reproduced in Freeman-Grenville, *East African Coast.*

4. "The Ancient History of Kilwa Kisiwani," in ibid., pp. 221–22.

5. de Barros, in ibid., pp. 89–90; "Arabic History of Kilwa Kisiwani," in ibid., pp. 36–37; and in S. A. Strong, trans. and ed., "The History of Kilwa," *Journal of the Royal Asiatic Society* 27 (1895): 387–88.

6. R. F. Burton, *Zanzibar: City, Island, and Coast* (London, 1872), 2: 362.

7. N. Chittick, "A New Look at the History of Pate," *JAH* 10 (1969): 382.

8. "The History of Pate," in Freeman-Grenville, *East African Coast,* pp. 242–43; cf. A. Werner, "A Swahili History of Pate," *Journal of the African Society* 14 (1914): 153–55.

9. al-Bakari al Lamuy, "Khabari Lamu," *Bantu Studies* 12 (1938): 9–13.

10. F. J. Berg, "The Swahili Community of Mombasa," *JAH* 9 (1968): 35–36.

11. A. C. Hollis, "Notes on the History of Vumba, East Africa," *JRAI* 30 (1900): 281–86; W. F. MacKay, "A Precolonial History of the Southern Kenya Coast" (Ph.D. thesis, Boston, 1975), pp. 56–68; J. M. Gray, "Zanzibar Local Histories," *Swahili* 30 (1959): 26.

12. T. M. Ricks, "Persian Gulf Seafaring and East Africa: Ninth to

Twelfth Centuries," *IJAHS* 3 (1970): 339–57; J. C. Wilkinson, "Oman and East Africa: New Light on Early Kilwan History from the Omani Sources," *IJAHS* 14 (1981): 272–305; J. de V. Allen, "The 'Shirazi' Problem in East African Coastal History," *Paideuma* 28 (1982): 9–28.

13. D. Nurse, "Bajuni Historical Linguistics," *Kenya Past and Present* 12 (1980): 34–43; Bujra, "Anthropological Study," p. 163.

14. Berg, "Mombasa," pp. 36, 45; MacKay, "Southern Kenya Coast," pp. 26–29; Burton, *Zanzibar*, 2: 362; C. Guillain, *Documents sur l'historie, la géographie, et le commerce de la côte orientale d'Afrique* (Paris, 1856), vol. 2, pt. 2: 240–41.

15. Ricks, "Persian Gulf Seafaring," p. 356n.

16. Caplan, *Choice and Constraint*, pp. 60–73; Amur Umar Sa'adi, "Mafia—Its History and Traditions," trans. D. Piggott, *TNR* 12 (1941): 23–27.

17. E. Saad, "Kilwa Dynastic Historiography," *History in Africa* 6 (1979): 181–83; Wilkinson, "Oman and East Africa."

Chapter 5: Rise of the Swahili Town-States, 1100–1500

1. M. Newitt, "The Southern Swahili Coast in the First Century of European Expansion," *Azania* 13 (1978): 111–26.

2. Yaqut, cited in J. S. Trimingham, *Islam in East Africa* (Oxford, 1964), pp. 5–6n.

3. Ibn Battuta, in Freeman-Grenville, *East African Coast*, pp. 27–32.

4. "Vasco da Gama's Return from India, 1499," in ibid., p. 57.

5. de Barros, in ibid., p. 78.

6. Duarte Barbosa, p. 134, and Monclaro, p. 142, both in ibid.

7. Horton, *Shanga 1980;* Chittick, "Excavations at Manda," p. 21.

8. al-Idrisi, in Freeman-Grenville, *East African Coast*, p. 20.

9. "Vasco da Gama's Discovery of East Africa for Portugal, 1498," in ibid., pp. 54–56.

10. "The Voyage of Pedro Alvares Cabral, 1500," in ibid., pp. 62–63.

11. Hans Mayr, in ibid., pp. 108–10.

12. Duarte Barbosa, in ibid., pp. 131–32.

13. Sassoon, "Excavations," pp. 16–41.

14. Duarte Barbosa, in Freeman-Grenville, *East African Coast*, p. 133. See also Chao Ju-Kua, ibid., p. 21; de Barros, ibid., p. 76; Monclaro, ibid., p. 139; and Yaqut, cited in Trimingham, *Islam*, p. 17.

15. Or Ngazija. See Shepherd, "Making of the Swahili," pp. 133–35.

16. Cabral, in Freeman-Grenville, *East African Coast*, p. 60.

17. Gaspar Correa, in ibid., p. 66. Contemporary population estimates for Kilwa range from 4,000 to 12,000, stated here.

18. de Barros, ibid., pp. 84–86; Mayr, ibid., pp. 106–8; Diego de Alcacova, ibid., pp. 123–24; Barbosa, ibid., p. 131; Monclaro, ibid., p. 138.

19. N. Chittick, "Kilwa: A Preliminary Report," *Azania* 1 (1966): 10–24; idem, *Kilwa*, 1:237–45.

20. Prins, *Didemic Lamu*, pp. 9–16, 38–56.

21. Zein, *Sacred Meadows*, pp. 11–164; J. de V. Allen, "The Swahili House: Culture and Ritual Concepts Underlying Its Plan and Structure," *AARP*, 1979, pp. 4–5; R. L. Pouwels, "The Medieval Foundations of East African Islam," *IJAHS* 11 (1978): 201–27, 393–409.

22. The following is taken from two sixteenth-century versions of the tradition—"The Arabic History of Kilwa," in Freeman-Grenville, *East African Coast*, pp. 34–49, and in Strong, "History of Kilwa," pp. 385–430; and an account collected by de Barros in 1505, in Freeman-Grenville, *East African Coast*, pp. 83–84, 89–93—as incisively interpreted by Saad, "Kilwa Dynastic Historiography," pp. 177–209. Saad's analysis of the tradition substantially modifies all previous interpretations, including that used by Chittick to interpret Kilwa archaeology (see n. 19, above). By establishing earlier origins for the Shirazi dynasty together with the indigenous nature of the succeeding Mahdali one, Saad clearly shows that change in Kilwa was continuous and evolutionary. Cf. Wilkinson, "Oman and East Africa," pp. 272–305.

23. J. de V. Allen, "The *Siwas* of Pate and Lamu: Two Antique Side-blown Horns from the Swahili Coast, *AARP* 9 (1976): 38–47.

24. "The History of Pate," in Freeman-Grenville, *East African Coast*, pp. 259–60.

25. G. S. P. Freeman-Grenville, *The French at Kilwa Island* (Oxford, 1965), p. 37.

26. Allen, *"Siwas,"* p. 46.

27. Trimingham, *Islam*, pp. 114–20; Lienhardt, *Medicine Man*, pp. 21–26, 52–62; R. Horton, "African Conversion," *Africa* 41 (1971): 101–8; Pouwels, "Islam and Islamic Leadership," pp. 142–97.

28. Two other areas of the possible impact of Islam on coastal society prior to the sixteenth century need to be explored. One is the effect of Muslim law on coastal politics and trade that might be revealed by a study of when various Muslim legal and commercial terms were adopted into Swahili. The other is the impact of literacy on coastal culture, for which we would need to know when Arabic script was first used to write Swahili and how extensive its use became over the following centuries. Evidence of the increasing role of Islam in coastal religious, commercial, and political life from the sixteenth to the nineteenth centuries is much more abundant, as shown in the detailed historical study by Randall Pouwels, "Islam and Islamic Leadership in the Coastal Communities of Eastern Africa, 1700–1914," and the modern survey by J. Spencer Trimingham, *Islam in East Africa*. Our evidence, together with that of these later studies, reveals a slow and syncretistic adoption of Islam, initially by a diaspora of traders, that closely parallels the spread of Islam in West Africa.

29. Caplan, *Choice and Constraint, in a Swahili Community*, pp. 84–

115; Pouwels, "Islam and Islamic Leadership," pp. 154–82; Lienhardt, *Medicine Man*, pp. 38–49.

30. Trimingham, *Islam*, p. 129.

31. T. H. Wilson, "Swahili Funerary Architecture of the North Kenyan Coast," *AARP*, 1979, pp. 33–34.

32. Hollis, "Notes on the History of Vumba," pp. 275–98.

BIBLIOGRAPHY

Abdallah Ali Nasir. *Al-Inkishafi, the Soul's Awakening.* Translated and edited by W. Hichens. Nairobi, 1972.

Abdulaziz, M. H. *Muyaka: Nineteenth Century Swahili Popular Poetry.* Nairobi, 1977.

Allen, J. de V. *Lamu Town: A Guide.* Mombasa, n.d.

──────. "The *Siwas* of Pate and Lamu: Two Antique Sideblown Horns from the Swahili Coast." *AARP* 9 (1976): 38–47.

──────. "Swahili Architecture in the Later Middle Ages." *African Arts* 7 (1974): 42–47, 66–68, 83–84.

──────. "Swahili Culture and the Nature of East Coast Settlement." *IJAHS* 14 (1981): 306–34.

──────. "Swahili Culture Reconsidered: Some Historical Implications of the Material Culture of the Northern Kenya Coast in the Eighteenth and Nineteenth Centuries." *Azania* 9 (1974): 105–38.

──────. "The Swahili House: Cultural and Ritual Concepts Underlying Its Plan and Structure." *AARP*, 1979, pp. 1–32.

──────. "Swahili Ornament: A Study of the Decoration of the Eighteenth Century Plasterwork and Carved Doors in the Lamu Region." *AARP* 3 (1973): 1–14; 4 (1973): 87–92.

──────. "Town and Country in Swahili Culture." In *Symposium Leo Frobenius*, pp. 298–316. Munich, 1974.

──────. "Traditional History and African Literature: The Swahili Case." *JAH* 23 (1982): 227–36.

Allen, J. de V., and T. H. Wilson, eds. "From Zinj to Zanzibar: Studies in History, Trade, and Society on the Eastern Coast of Africa." *Paideuma* 28 (1982).

Alpers, E. A. "Muqdisho in the Nineteenth Century: A Regional Perspective." *JAH* 24 (1983): 441–59.

Amur Umar Sa'adi. "Mafia—Its History and Traditions." Translated by D. Piggott. *TNR* 12 (1941): 23–27.

al-Bakari al Lamuy. "Khabari Lamu." *Bantu Studies* 12 (1938): 3–33.

Baker, E. C. "Notes on the Shirazi of East Africa." *TNR* 11 (1941): 1–10.

Berg, F. J. "The Swahili Community of Mombasa, 1500–1900." *JAH* 9 (1968): 35–56.

Berg, F. J., and B. J. Walter. "Mosques, Population, and Urban Development in Mombasa." *Hadith* 1 (1968): 47–100.

Bujra, J. M. "An Anthropological Study of Political Action in a Bajuni Village in Kenya." Ph.D. thesis, London, 1968.

Bunger, R. L. *Islamization among the Upper Pokomo.* Syracuse, 1973.

Burton, R. F. *The Lake Regions of Central Africa.* London, 1860.

————. *Zanzibar: City, Island, and Coast.* London, 1872.

Caplan, A. P. *Choice and Constraint in a Swahili Community.* London, 1975.

————. "Gender, Ideology, and Modes of Production on the East Coast of Africa." *Paideuma* 28 (1982): 29–43.

Cassanelli, L. V. *The Shaping of Somali Society.* Philadelphia, 1982.

Cerulli, E. *Somalia: Scritti vari Editi Ed Inediti.* Rome, 1957.

Chamanga, M. A., and N.-J. Geunier. *Le Dictionnaire comorien-français et français-comorien du R. P. Sacleux.* Paris, 1979.

Chittick, N. "The Book of the Zanj." Manuscript.

————. "The Book of the Zenj and the Mijikenda." *IJAHS* 9 (1976): 68–73.

————. "Discoveries in the Lamu Archipelago." *Azania* 2 (1967): 37–68.

————. *Kilwa: An Islamic Trading City on the East African Coast.* Nairobi, 1974.

————. "Kilwa and the Arab Settlements on the East African Coast." *JAH* 4 (1963): 179–90.

————. "Kilwa: A Preliminary Report." *Azania* 1 (1966): 1–36.

————. *Kisimani Mafia.* Dar es Salaam, 1961.

————. "Manda and the Immigration of the Shirazi." Institute of African Studies, Nairobi, 1979, paper 119.

————. "Mediaeval Mogadishu." *Paideuma* 28 (1982): 45–62.

————. "A New Look at the History of Pate." *JAH* 10 (1969): 375–91.

————. "Report on Excavations at Manda, 1978." *Nyame Akuma* 14 (1979): 20–22.

————. "The 'Shirazi' Colonization of East Africa." *JAH* 6 (1965): 275–94.

————. "Unguja Ukuu: The Earliest Imported Pottery and an Abbasid Dinar." *Azania* 1 (1966): 161–63.

Chittick, N., and R. I. Rotberg, eds. *East Africa and the Orient.* New York, 1975.

Coupland, R. *East Africa and Its Invaders.* Oxford, 1938.

Dalby, D. "The Prehistorical Explication of Guthrie's *Comparative Bantu, Part II: Interpretation of Cultural Vocabulary.*" *JAH* 17 (1976): 1–27.

Darroch, R. G. "Some Notes on the Early History of the Tribes Living on the Lower Tana, collected by Mikael Samson and Others." *Journal of the East Africa and Uganda Natural History Society* 17 (1943/44): 244–54, 370–94.

Deed, F. *Giryama-English Dictionary.* Nairobi, 1964.

Dickson, T. A. "The Regalia of the Wa-Vumba." *Man* 21 (1921): 33–35.

Eastman, C. M. "Who Are the Waswahili?" *Africa* 41 (1971): 228–36.

Eastman, C. M., and F. M. Topan. "The Siu: Notes on the People and Their Language." *Swahili* 36 (1966): 22–48.

Ehret, C. *Ethiopians and East Africans.* Nairobi, 1974.

————. "Historical Inferences from Transformation in Cultural Vocabulary." *SUGIA* 2 (1980): 189–218.

————. *The Historical Reconstruction of Southern Cushitic Phonology and Vocabulary.* Berlin, 1980.

————. "Patterns of Bantu and Central Sudanic Settlements in Central and Southern Africa." *Transafrican Journal of History* 3 (1973): 1–71.

————. *Southern Nilotic History.* Evanston, Ill., 1971.

Ehret, C., and M. Posnansky, eds. *The Archaeological and Linguistic Reconstruction of African History.* San Francisco, 1982.

Esmail, Z. "Towards a History of Islam in East Africa." *Kenya Historical Review* 3 (1975): 147–58.

Fadiman, J. "Early History of the Meru of Mt. Kenya." *JAH* 14 (1973): 9–27.

Freeman-Grenville, G. S. P. *The East African Coast: Select Documents from the First Century to the Early Nineteenth Century.* Oxford, 1962.

————. *The French at Kilwa Island.* Oxford, 1965.

————. "Medieval Evidences for Swahili." *Journal of the East African Swahili Committee* 29 (1959): 10–23.

————. *The Medieval History of the Coast of Tanganyika.* London, 1962.

————. "Swahili Literature and the History and Archaeology of the East African Coast." *Journal of the East African Swahili Committee* 28 (1958): 7–25.

Garlake, P. S. *The Early Islamic Architecture of the East African Coast.* Nairobi, 1966.

Ghaidan, U. *Lamu: A Study in Conservation.* Nairobi, n.d.

————. *Lamu: A Study of the Swahili Town.* Nairobi, 1975.

Gray, J. M. "The Hadimu and Tumbatu of Zanzibar." *TNR* 81/82 (1977): 135–53.

————. "A History of Kilwa." *TNR* 31 (1951): 1–28; 32 (1952): 11–37.

————. *History of Zanzibar from the Middle Ages to 1856.* London, 1962.

————. "Zanzibar Local Histories." *Swahili* 30 (1959): 24–50; 31 (1960): 111–39.

Grottanelli, V. L. *Pescatori dell'Oceano Indiano.* Rome, 1955.

Guenier, N.-J., ed. *Si Mimi Mwongo Watu wa Zamani: Contes en dialecte Swahili du village Marodoka (Madagascar).* Zanzibar, 1980.

Guillain, C. *Documents sur l'historie, la géographie, et le commerce de la côte orientale d'Afrique.* Paris, 1856.

Guthrie, M. *Comparative Bantu.* Vol. 2. Farnsworth, Eng., 1971.

Gwynne, M. D. "The Origin and Spread of Some Domestic Food Plants of East Africa." In Chittick and Rotberg, *East Africa and the Orient.*

Haji Chum. "A Vocabulary of the Kikae Dialect." *Swahili* 33 (1962/63): 51–68.

Harries, L. *Swahili Poetry.* Oxford, 1962.

Heine, B. "Bemerkungen zur-Boni Sprache (Kenia)." *Afrika und Ubersee* 60 (1977): 245–95.

———. "The Sam Languages: A History of Rendille, Boni, and Somali." *Afroasiatic Linguistics* 6 (1978): 1–93.

Heine, B.; F. Rottland; and R. Vossen. "Proto-Baz: Some Aspects of Early Nilotic-Cushitic Contact." *SUGIA* 1 (1979): 75–92.

———. "Some Cultural Evidence of the Early Sam-speaking People of Eastern Africa." *SUGIA* 3 (1981): 169–200.

Hill, T. "The Primary Dialects of Swahili: An Approach to a Linguistic-Geographical Survey, Part I." *Kiswahili* 43 (1973): 7–18.

Hinnebusch, T. "Swahili: Genetic Affiliations and Evidence." *Studies in African Linguistics*, supp. 6 (1976): 95–108.

———. "The Shungwaya Hypothesis: A Linguistic Reappraisal." In J. T. Gallagher, ed., *East African Culture History*. Syracuse, 1976.

Hinnebusch, T.; D. Nurse; and M. Mould. *Studies in the Classification of Eastern Bantu Languages*. Hamburg: SUGIA, 1982.

Hollis, A. C. "Notes on the History of Vumba, East Africa." *JRAI* 30 (1900): 275–98.

Horton, M. *Shanga 1980*. Cambridge, 1980.

Kirkman, J. S. *The Arab City of Gedi*. London, 1964.

———. *Fort Jesus*. London, 1974.

———. *Men and Monuments of the East African Coast*. London, 1964.

———. *The Palace*. The Hague, 1963.

———. *Ungwana on the Tana*. The Hague, 1966.

Krapf, L., and J. Rebmann. *A Nika-English Dictionary*. London, 1889.

Krumm, B. *Woerter und Wortformen orientalischen Ursprungs im Swahili*. Hamburg, 1932.

Lambert, H. E. *Chi-Chifundi: A Dialect of the Southern Kenya Coast*. Kampala, 1958.

———. *Chi-Jomvu and Ki-Ngare*. Kampala, 1958.

———. *Ki-Vumba: A Dialect of the Southern Kenya Coast*. Kampala, 1957.

Lewcock, R. "Architectural Connections between Africa and Parts of the Indian Ocean Littoral." *AARP* 9 (1976): 13–23.

Lienhardt, P. "A Controversy over Islamic Custom in Kilwa Kivinge, Tanzania." In I. M. Lewis, ed., *Islam in Tropical Africa*, pp. 374–86. London, 1966.

———. *The Medicine Man*. Oxford, 1968.

———. "The Mosque College of Lamu and Its Social Background." *TNR* 53 (1959): 228–42.

MacKay, W. F. "A Precolonial History of the Southern Kenya Coast." Ph.D. thesis, Boston, 1975.

Martin, B. G. "Arab Migrations to East Africa in Medieval Times." *IJAHS* 7 (1974): 367–90.

Metzler, M. "The Near East and East Africa: An Initial Investigation into

Settlement Patterns through Ceramic Dating." University of Nairobi, Department of History seminar paper, 1978.

Midani bin Mwidad. "The Founding of Rabai." Translated and edited by L. Harries. *Swahili* 31 (1960): 140–49.

Middleton, J., and J. Campbell. *Zanzibar: Its Society and Politics.* London, 1965.

Miehe, G. *Die Sprache der Aelteren Swahili-Dichtung.* Berlin, 1979.

Miller, J. C., ed. *The African Past Speaks.* Folkestone, 1980.

Newitt, M. "The Southern Swahili Coast in the First Century of European Expansion." *Azania* 13 (1978): 111–26.

Nicholls, C. S. *The Swahili Coast.* London, 1971.

Nurse, D. "Bajuni Historical Linguistics." *Kenya Past and Present* 12 (1980): 34–43.

————— . "Bantu Migration into East Africa: Linguistic Evidence." In Ehret and Posnansky, *Archaeological and Linguistic Reconstruction.*

————— . *Classification of the Chaga Dialects.* Hamburg, 1979.

————— . "Is Comorian Swahili? Being an Examination of the Diachronic Relationship between Comorian and Coastal Swahili." Round Table on the Limits of Swahili, Paris, 1983.

————— . "On Dating Swahili." *Etudes Ocean Indien* 2 (1983): 59–72.

————— . "A Historical View of the Southern Dialects of Swahili." *SUGIA* 6 (1984).

————— . "History from Linguistics: The Case of the Tana River." *History in Africa* 10 (1983).

————— . "A Hypothesis Concerning the Origin of Swahili." *Azania* 18 (1983).

————— . "Linguistic Evidence for Shungwaya." First International Congress of Somali Studies, Muqdisho, 1980.

————— . "The Proto-Sabaki Verb System and Its Subsequent Development." *SUGIA* 5 (1983).

————— . "Segeju and Daisu: A Case Study of Evidence from Oral Tradition and Comparative Linguistics." *History in Africa* 9 (1982): 175–208.

————— . "The Swahili Dialects of Somalia and the Northern Kenya Coast." In M.-F. Rombi, ed., *Etudes sur le Bantu oriental,* pp. 73–121. Paris, 1982.

————— . "A Tentative Classification of the Primary Dialects of Swahili." *SUGIA* 4 (1982): 165–205.

Nurse, D., and C. Ehret. "The Taita Cushites." *SUGIA* 3 (1981): 125–68.

Nurse, D., and G. Philippson. "The Bantu Languages of East Africa: A Lexicostatistical Survey." In E. C. Polome, ed., *Language In Tanzania.* London, 1980.

————— . "Historical Implications of the Language Map of East Africa." In L. Bouquiaux, ed., *L'Expansion Bantoue.* Paris, 1980.

Ogot, B. A., ed. *Kenya Before 1900.* Nairobi, 1976.

————— , ed. *Zamani.* Nairobi, 1973.

Ohly, R. "Dating of Swahili Language." *Kiswahili* 42 (1973): 10–23.

Omari bin Stamboul. "An Early History of Mombasa and Tanga." Translated by E. C. Becker. *TNR* 31 (1951): 32–36.

Pearce, F. B. *Zanzibar.* London, 1920.

Phillipson, D. W. *The Later Prehistory of Eastern and Southern Africa.* London, 1977.

————. "Some Iron Age Sites in the Lower Tana Valley." *Azania* 14 (1979): 155–62.

Polome, E. C. "The Earliest Attestations of Swahili." Mimeographed. N.d.

Polome, E. C., and C. P. Hill, eds. *Language in Tanzania.* London, 1980.

Pouwels, R. L. "Islam and Islamic Leadership in the Coastal Communities of Eastern Africa, 1700–1914." Ph.D. thesis, Los Angeles, 1979.

————. "The Medieval Foundations of East African Islam." *IJAHS* 11 (1978): 201–27, 393–409.

————. "Tenth Century Settlement of the East African Coast: The Case for Qarmatian/Isma'ili Connections." *Azania* 9 (1974): 65–74.

Prins, A. H. J. *Didemic Lamu.* Groningen, 1971.

————. *Sailing from Lamu.* Assen, 1965.

————. *The Swahili-speaking Peoples of Zanzibar and the East African Coast.* London, 1967.

Richardson, J. *A New Malagasy-English Dictionary.* Tananarive, 1885.

Ricks, T. M. "Persian Gulf Seafaring and East Africa: Ninth to Twelfth Centuries." *IJAHS* 3 (1970): 339–57.

Robinson, A. E. "The Shirazi Colonisation of East Africa." *TNR* 3 (1937): 40–81; 7 (1939): 92–112.

Rollestone, I. H. O. "The Watumbatu of Zanzibar." *TNR* 8 (1939).

Rombi, M.-F. *Premiers éléments pour une description du parler Mahorais de la langue Comorienne.* Paris, 1979.

Rombi, M.-F., and M. A. Chamanga. *Contes Comoriens.* Paris, 1980.

Rzewuski, E. *Vocabulario da lingua Mwani.* Maputo, 1979.

Saad, E. "Kilwa Dynastic Historiography." *History in Africa* 6 (1979): 177–209.

Sacleux, C. *Dictionnaire swahili-français.* Paris, 1939.

Said Bakari bin Sultani Ahmed. *The Swahili Chronicle of Ngazija.* Translated and edited by L. Harries. Bloomington, Ind., 1977.

Salim, A. E. *The Swahili-speaking Peoples of Kenya's Coast, 1895–1945.* Nairobi, 1973.

Sassoon, H. "Excavations at the Site of Early Mombasa." *Azania* 15 (1980): 1–44.

Schaffer, L. "A Historiographic Appraisal of Kenyan Coastal History." *Ufahamu* 9 (1979): 61–77.

Shariff, I. N. "Waswahili and Their Language: Some Misconceptions." *Kiswahili* 43 (1973): 67–75.

Shepherd, G. M. "The Making of the Swahili: A View from the Southern End of the East African Coast." *Paideuma* 28 (1982): 129–48.

———— . "Two Marriage Forms in the Comoro Islands: An Investigation."
Africa 47 (1977): 344–59.

Sheriff, A. M. H. "The Rise of a Commercial Empire: An Aspect of the
Economic History of Zanzibar, 1770–1873." Ph.D. thesis, London, 1971.

———— . "Trade and Underdevelopment: The Role of International Trade
in the Economic History of the East African Coast before the Sixteenth
Century." *Hadith* 5 (1975): 1–23.

Sinclair, P. "Chibuene: An Early Trading Site in Southern Mozambique."
Paideuma 28 (1982): 149–64.

Skene, R. "Arab and Swahili Dances and Ceremonies." *JRAI* 47 (1917): 413–
34.

Soper, R. C. "Bantu Migration into East Africa: Archaeological Evidence."
In Ehret and Posnansky, *Archaeological and Linguistic Reconstruction.*

———— . "Iron Age Archaeology and Traditional History in Embu, Mbeere,
and Chuka Areas of Central Kenya." *Azania* 14 (1979): 31–60.

———— . "Kwale: An Early Iron Age Site in Southeastern Kenya." *Azania*
2 (1967): 1–18.

Spear, T. *The Kaya Complex: A History of the Mijikenda Peoples of the Kenya
Coast to 1900.* Nairobi, 1978.

———— . *Kenya's Past.* London, 1981.

———— . "Oral Traditions: Whose History?" *History in Africa* 8 (1981):
163–79.

———— . "The Shirazi in Swahili Traditions, Culture, and History." *History in Africa* 11 (1984).

———— . *Traditions of Origin and Their Interpretation.* Athens, 1982.

Stigand, C. H. *Land of Zinj.* London, 1913.

Stiles, D. "A History of the Hunting Peoples of the Northern East African
Coast." *Paideuma* 28 (1982): 165–74.

———— . "Hunters of the Northern East African Coast: Origins and Historical Processes." *Africa* 51 (1981): 848–62.

Strandes, J. *The Portuguese Period in East Africa.* Nairobi, 1961.

Strobel, M. *Muslim Women in Mombasa.* New Haven, 1979.

———— . "Women's Wedding Celebrations in Mombasa, Kenya." *African
Studies Review* 18 (1975): 35–45.

Strong, S. A., trans. and ed. "The History of Kilwa." *Journal of the Royal
Asiatic Society* 27 (1895): 385–430.

Swartz, M. J. "Religious Courts, Community, and Ethnicity among the Swahili of Mombasa: An Historical Study of Social Boundaries." *Africa* 49
(1979): 29–41.

Tolmacheva, M. "The Arabic Influence on Swahili Literature: A Historian's
View." *Journal of African Studies* 5 (1978): 223–43.

———— . "The Origin of the Name 'Swahili.' " *TNR* 77/78 (1976): 27–37.

———— . " 'They Came from Damascus in Syria': A Note on Traditional
Lamu Historiography." *IJAHS* 12 (1979): 259–69.

———— . "The Zanj Language." *Kiswahili* 45 (1975): 16–24.

Trimingham, J. S. *Islam in East Africa*. Oxford, 1964.

Turton, E. R. "Bantu, Galla, and Somali Migration in the Horn of Africa: A Reassessment of the Juba/Tana Area." *JAH* 16 (1975): 519–37.

Van Otterloo, K., and R. Van Otterloo. *A Sociolinguistics Study: The Bantu Language Groups of the Kenya Coastal Area*. Nairobi, 1980.

Velten, E. *Desturi za Waswahili*. Göttingen, 1905.

————. *Prosa und Poesie der Suaheli*. Berlin, 1907.

Villers, A. *Sons of Sinbad*. New York, 1940.

Werner, A. "Swahili History of Pate." *Journal of the African Society* 14 (1914): 148–61, 278–97, 392–413.

————. "The Swahili Saga of Liongo Fumo." *Bulletin of the School of Oriental and African Studies* 4 (1926–28): 247–55.

Whiteley, W. H. *The Dialects and Verse of Pemba*. Kampala, 1958.

————. "An Introduction to the Rural Dialects of Zanzibar, Part I." *Swahili* 30 (1959): 41–69.

————. *Ki-Mtang'ata: A Dialect of the Mrima Coast, Tanganyika*. Kampala, 1956.

————. "Kimvita." *Journal of the East African Swahili Committee* 25 (1955): 10–39.

————. *Language in Kenya*. London, 1974.

————. *Swahili: The Rise of a National Language*. London, 1969.

Wilkinson, J. C. "Oman and East Africa: New Light on Early Kilwan History from the Omani Sources." *IJAHS* 14 (1981): 272–305.

Wilson, T. H. *The Monumental Architecture and Archaeology of the Central and Southern Kenya Coast*. Nairobi, 1980.

————. *The Monumental Architecture and Archaeology North of the Tana River*. Nairobi, 1978.

————. "Settlement Patterns on the Coast of Southern Somalia and Kenya." First International Congress of Somali Studies, Muqdisho, 1980.

————. "Spatial Analysis and Settlement Patterns on the East African Coast." *Paideuma* 28 (1982): 201–19.

————. "Swahili Funerary Architecture of the North Kenya Coast." *AARP*, 1979, pp. 33–46.

Ylvisaker, M. H. *Lamu in the Nineteenth Century*. Boston, 1979.

Zein, A. el. *The Sacred Meadows*. Evanston, Ill., 1974.

Index

University of Pennsylvania Press

The Ethnohistory Series

Lee V. Cassanelli, Juan A. Villamarin, and Judith E. Villamarin, Editors

Ronald Atkinson. *The Roots of Ethnicity: The Origins of the Acholi of Uganda Before 1800.* 1994

Christopher Boehm. *Blood Revenge: The Enactment and Management of Conflict in Montenegro and Other Tribal Societies.* 1987

Lee V. Cassanelli. *The Shaping of Somali Society: Reconstructing the History of a Pastoral People, 1600-1900.* 1982

James L. Giblin. *The Politics of Environmental Control in Northeastern Tanzania, 1840-1940.* 1992

Robert M. Hill II and John Monaghan. *Continuities in Highland Maya Social Organization: Ethnohistory in Sacapulas, Guatemala.* 1987

Maria L. Lagos. *Class and Culture: The Transformation of Agrarian Social Relations in Cochabamba, Bolivia.* 1994

James McCann. *From Poverty to Famine in Northeast Ethiopia: A Rural History, 1900-1935.* 1987

Derek Nurse and Thomas Spear. *The Swahili: Reconstructing the History and Language of an African Society, 800-1500.* 1985

James A. Quirin. *The Evolution of the Ethiopian Jews: A History of the Beta Israel (Falasha) to 1920.* 1992

Norman B. Schwartz. *Forest Society: A Social History of Petén, Guatemala.* 1990

Lawrence J. Taylor. *Dutchmen on the Bay: The Ethnohistory of a Contractual Community.* 1983